Struggling to Be Holy

Struggling to Be Holy

JUDY HIRST

DARTON · LONGMAN + TODD

To John, James and Beth who have struggled alongside me and struggled because of me but loved me none the less.

First published in 2006 by
Darton, Longman and Todd Ltd
1 Spencer Court
140–142 Wandsworth High Street
London SW18 4JJ

Reprinted 2007

ISBN 10: 0-232-52435-4
ISBN 13: 978-0-232-52435-6

A catalogue record for this book is available from the British Library.

Designed and produced by Sandie Boccacci
Phototypeset in 12/15pt Garamond
Printed and bound in Great Britain by
The Cromwell Press, Trowbridge, Wiltshire

Contents

Acknowledgements

That I should write a book is unlikely and no one could be more surprised than me at this turn of events! I am indebted to the Revd Dr Steve Croft who, while he was Warden at Cranmer Hall, heard something in the talks I gave to the community which led him to encourage me to write. I am also very grateful to St John's College for allowing me to have a period of study leave, and to my colleagues for taking on the extra work which enabled me to do this.

Crucially, I need to acknowledge the people with whom I share my life, many of whom have also walked alongside me in the writing of this book. I have been fortunate all my life to be able to share it with a loving family, friends and colleagues and it is through interaction and conversation with them that I have gained whatever small kernel of Christian maturity I have. Many of them have put up with endless questions and conversation about whatever topic was in hand and I am aware that this book reflects a shared wisdom which I have been privileged to express.

Ruth Etchells believed in the book from the start and has accompanied me throughout, spurring me on when I was dejected and would have given up, and she has been the most delightful and encouraging companion at all times. What a privilege to have such a wise mentor for whom I thank God and from whom I have learned so much. Deep thanks are due to all those who read parts of this book and provided me with invaluable insights, wisdom and questions: Rob Croft, Carol

Simmons, Paul Waterfield, Sue and John Lambert, Anna Matthews, John Pritchard, Fiona Lingard, Christine Wilkinson, Peter Shaw and David Bosworth. I am equally indebted to Helen Hornby for her sterling efforts with both punctuation and grammar to make my manuscript intelligible.

I have also been privileged to work with many people in the more professional relationship of counsellor, priest or spiritual director. I have drawn on these shared experiences in the book, and am grateful for those who have given me permission to use their stories and for their willingness to share them in this way.

Throughout life we receive wisdom and insight in numbers of ways both from people and in what we read. Among those people, I am conscious of three who have particularly shared my journey of faith. Alison Marshall has been my friend since childhood, and through her generous sharing of insights, experience and books has informed this book more than any other person, and Sister Imelda Poole IBVM and Gordon Smith, who as spiritual director and counsellor, have walked the way with me and shown me so much of the love and acceptance of God. In addition to helpful conversations with people there have been writers whose insights have seeped into my consciousness. I would particularly like to acknowledge the writings of: J. V. Taylor, Henri Nouwen, Richard Rohr, David Ford, Michael Mayne, Trevor Dennis, Philip Sheldrake and Maria Boulding.

Finally, thanks also to my editor Virginia Hearn, who nursed this book through its three years of emerging; encouraging and caring for the flagging writer and never asking where we were going until we got there! Thanks also to St Anthony's Priory in Durham who gave me a safe, quiet and uninterrupted space in which to write the initial draft and to

Kate Bruce for giving me study space in the closing stages and for helping me with the final draft.

I am so grateful that the Christian journey is not one which we make alone. This book is a way of saying thank you, not least to my husband and children who have discovered that writing a book makes me even more challenging to live with than usual!

The publishers wish to thank the following for the use of copyright material:

Ann Lewin for 'Revelation', taken from *Watching for the Kingfisher* (published by Inspire, an imprint of Methodist Publishing House); A P Watt Ltd on behalf of Michael B Yeats for extracts from 'He Wishes for the Cloths of Heaven' by W B Yeats; A P Watt Ltd on behalf of The National Trust for Places of Historic Interest or Natural Beauty for extracts from 'If' by Rudyard Kipling; J. M. Dent, a division of The Orion Publishing Group, for 'The Bright Field' and 'Pilgrimages' taken from *Collected Poems* by R. S. Thomas; Methodist Publishing House for the Covenant Prayer, taken from the *Methodist Worship Book*, © Trustees for Methodist Church purposes; Restoration Music Ltd for extracts from 'As the Deer' by Martin Nystrom, © copyright 1983 Restoration Music Ltd/Sovereign Music UK, PO Box 356, Leighton Buzzard, LU7 3WP, UK. Reproduced by permission; Ruth Etchells for 'The Judas Ballad' to be published in *The Rainbow Coloured Cross* (SPCK, 2007); The Archbishops' Council for the Prayer of Absolution from *Common Worship: Services and Prayers for the Church of England*, copyright © The Archbishops' Council 2000.

Foreword

'Holiness' is one of those rare and lovely words in our religious vocabulary which has not yet been either sentimentalised or over-colonised. As a concept it still has great drawing power in the (often secret) longing of many, who both revere holiness where they see it in others, and yearn to grow in it themselves.

However, an unfortunate consequence of this continuing reverence for holiness is that many fear this is something beyond them, not really for 'ordinary' Christians; and sadly this fear can be increased by some of the literature of holiness, which submerges the living and simple beauty of its subject in a sacral language which often feels esoteric and sometimes, alas, pretentious.

And so what joy to have in Judy Hirst a writer on holiness who declares in her very title her complete rejection of cornering her subject as a specialist achiever. Instead she draws us into a fresh and hopeful way through her witty and moving account of her own *struggles* to be holy. And what joy, too, to find in her introduction such a reassurance as this:

> Holiness is much less about self-discipline than it is about learning to entrust yourself to the God who

> loves you. It is about taking the risk of allowing God to interact with the truth of ourselves, no strings attached.

My guess is that reassurance will be the first and continuing experience of many as they delightedly read on in this unputdownable book. But part of its power is that because one *is* reassured, one is also enabled to take risks. So we learn to face truths about ourselves not wrapped up in a safely distancing 'special' language, but spelled out with gloriously self-deprecating humour in the language of everyday life:

> Holiness is about God being present and our being present to God ... the problem is to be present ourselves. God is there, but where are we?

So 'allowing God to interact with the *truth* of ourselves' with humour rather than despair, *because God loves us*, is the urgent message of this book. ('God loves me,' Judy says in the first reflection, 'Hiding from God', 'but I live as though he's out to get me.') And each reflection looks very practically at how this might be tackled in areas of our lives we all struggle with: desires; forgiving; paying attention; friendship; success and failure. In each reflection there are nuggets of pure gold which I suspect will become part of the sayings of the twenty-first-century church, quoted everywhere and their attribution soon lost. So remember you read them first in this book! Here are a few samples:

> We are made in the image of God who knows desire and who desires us.
>
> All other desires will find their right place if they are contained within God's desire for us and ours for him.
>
> God can live with the reality that we are sinners even if we find it hard to do so.
>
> The only person qualified to throw the stone chooses not to.
>
> Christianity is not a magic formula: it is a relationship.

I have had the privilege of knowing Judy for many years. Rather like the apostle Paul, she is in worldly terms very highly qualified to write on such struggles of the human spirit, both academically and in terms of her career and her present post. But, again like Paul, she has chosen instead to root the explorations of these pages in her deepening personal experience of God's love over these years, and what, gently but insistently, through both tears and laughter, this has been drawing her to understand of

> the place where everything is possible, the place of holiness … discovering that we can be at home in ourselves and that God is and always has been at home there with us.

And so she has not written a book about theories of holiness, or its history (though her range of reference, light though its touch, is very rich).

I had the privilege of watching the book grow. When I read it in its final form I wanted both to laugh and cry, because it is not simply a marvellous aid in the pathway of holiness – it is also *itself* full of holiness: penitent and joyful; this-worldly and other-worldly; humanly commonsense-full and yet full of that divinely possible holiness.

Read it! And perhaps you will be surprised to discover how far along the pathway of holiness God has already drawn you.

Ruth Etchells

Prologue

It was a mystery to me and an uncomfortable one at that. How had I got into the situation where I had offered to write a book on holiness? *Struggling to Be Holy* was the exact title that I had given to the council of the theological college in Durham where I teach pastoral ministry, accompanied as I recall with a quip about knowing rather more about struggling than about being holy! Now the chips were down, for today I was to meet with a potential editor and I still had no idea what I was going to say to her. I had set aside the morning to think but the door bell had rung and a very distressed young woman was there to see me. She had been abused as a child and, whilst usually coping well, occasionally found herself in a very painful place. There is never much that can be said at such times. All that really helps is to be with her and to hold her as she cries. So that was how the morning passed and no thinking was done. Lunchtime found me dashing to the meeting with a sinking feeling in my heart. How had I got myself into this embarrassing position? In exasperation, I said out loud to myself, 'I don't know anything about holiness!' and it was as if a voice asked, 'So what have you just been doing?' I was blank for a moment until I remembered the morning of sitting with someone in pain. 'Isn't that something about holiness then?' the voice replied.

This stopped me in my tracks because it had never really occurred to me that caring for someone in need was about holiness. I suppose over the years, I had gathered the impression that someone like me was not holy. Holiness was about being contained and controlled, about keeping silent for weeks, about taking yourself away from people to be on your own. It was about being serene, peaceful, wise and devout and being endowed with extreme purity. Holiness had often seemed to be a quality which was acquired by strict discipline and effort and the ones most likely to be successful in the Christian life those who were rigidly self-controlled and ordered and who could seamlessly be quiet, retreat, keep the commandments, attend church frequently and so on! However, writing this book has made it very clear to me that holiness is much less about developing self-discipline than it is about learning to entrust yourself to the God who loves you. It is about taking the risk of allowing God to interact with the truth of ourselves, no strings attached. So those who think they have success in the Christian life may actually be at the most risk.

Every year, an enthusiastic new group of students arrive in Durham to train for the ordained ministry. They have jumped through many hoops to get there and have been thoroughly assessed in every aspect of their lives. Many come with established patterns of prayer and devotion and very soon discover that for a whole range of reasons training for ordained ministry damages their devotional health! People, understandably, get annoyed and upset that their disciplined and ordered approaches to God have gone awry. I have become increasingly certain over the years that God is nowhere near as anxious about this as they are, for it is all too easy to avoid real encounter with God through religious practice. As the success and often illusion of these structures are removed the ordinands are left to work out their relationship with God in this new context. The key thing is about sticking at this relationship when all the external props of established practice are removed. It is about being brought again to that place of utter dependency. As Metropolitan Anthony of Sourozh put it so well,

> First of all, it is very important to remember that prayer is an encounter and a relationship, a relationship which is deep, and this relationship cannot be forced either on us or on God. If we could mechanically draw him into an encounter, force him to meet us, simply because we have chosen this moment to meet him, there would be no relationship and no encounter. We can do that with an image, with the imagination, or with the various idols we can put in front of us instead of God; we can do nothing of that sort with the living God, any more than we can do it with a living person.[1]

In Luke's gospel we are told that Jesus is aiming the Parable of the Tax Collector and the Pharisee exactly at people who were complacently pleased about how they were doing in the religious life.[2] As they come to pray the Pharisee lists his achievements: his moral behaviour, his fasting and his tithing, but the tax collector slumps down in utter despair and defeat and says only, 'God, be merciful to me, a sinner!' It is him rather than the Pharisee with whom God can do business. If you come to God simply as you are, hiding nothing (Reflection 1), then God will help you to become more fully yourself. The Pharisee, however, is so taken up with himself that there is no care for the tax collector and definitely no spare capacity for an encounter with the God whom he is addressing!

Holiness is about God being present and our being present to God. The more we can be in honest relationship with God, the holier we will become. Some Christians behave as if the task is to persuade God to be with them, but the delightful truth is that he is already present in the relationship. The problem is to be present ourselves. God is there but where are we? I have an older friend whom I love to bits and to whom I am indebted for many things. She has inspired me and encouraged me in the Christian life by both her wisdom and her delightful sense of humour and has been a great source of practical help in my ministry. However, this was not always the case. Our first meeting was at a college lunch. Beth, my daughter, was a tiny baby who was being uncharacteristically grumpy and I was feeling exhausted and inadequate. A mutual friend introduced me to Marian who is an experienced psychiatrist and was, at that time, doing some work on the interface between depression and theology. 'You're a counsellor, so I'm sure you'll have a lot in common,' was the cheery introduction. All that I actually had in common was that I already felt depressed and the thought of making intelligent conversation with this rather bright and scary woman was only serving to make me more depressed. I felt inadequate and I shied away. Fortunately, I got a second chance, as Marian was to be on the management group for my job as the Bishop's Advisor in Pastoral Care and Counselling. Initially, I was still suspicious and insecure but gradually trust grew. It was my defensiveness and fear that blocked the relationship as is so often the case between God and us. It was a question of trust and as I have grown to trust her she has been able to make a significant impact on my life and faith.

So God is in us already and it is we who have to learn to live creatively with him. This takes some considerable practice! We cannot make ourselves holy whatever effort we expend. What we need to be is as open as we can to the holiness which is within each of us. We need to allow God to give himself to us, even though we are not worthy, and through the experience of unconditional love and forgiveness (Reflection 3) we will be changed. The success of the venture is that we will become our real, best selves and this involves a different journey for each of us. There is a good illustration of this in Rowan Williams' book *Silence and Honey Cakes* about one of the desert fathers:

> There was a monk who complained that Abba Arsenius was not renowned for physical asceticism; the old man dealing with this asks the complainant what he had done before becoming a monk. He had worked as a shepherd sleeping on the ground, eating sparse meals of gruel; Arsenius had been tutor to the imperial family and slept between sheets of silk. In other words, the simplicity of the desert life represented no very great change for the censorious observer but a different world for Arsenius.[3]

It is so important to keep this particularity in mind as we struggle to be holy. Since I was a child I have always been attracted to the idea of the 'Caucus-race' in *Alice in Wonderland.* It is a crazy race which both starts and finishes unpredictably with the consequence that no one has any idea who has won. I think it appealed to my sense of the anarchic! When they all crowd round asking the Dodo who has won he finally, after much thought, pronounces that, '*Everybody* has won, and all must have prizes.'[4] I am privileged to have a number of close friends, but the relationship with each one is unique, giving me different gifts, confronting me with different challenges. So it is that each walk with God is unique, what is a challenge for one of us will not be an issue for another. The challenge and opportunity for all of us, however, is to enter into a relationship with the living God which will help us to become more fully the person whom we hold the potential to be:

> On his deathbed Rabbi Zuscha was asked what he thought life beyond the grave would be like. The old man thought for a long time: then he replied: 'I don't really know. But one thing I do know: when I get there I am not going to be asked "Why weren't you Moses?" Or "Why weren't you David?" I am going to be asked "Why weren't you Zuscha?"'[5]

When we choose to be ourselves in free relationship to God, not to conform to the expectations of others, we choose life with all its joys and disappointments. We choose to be all that we are, with all that is delightful and all that is damaged. After many years of struggle within myself, I eventually delivered myself to a counsellor. I wanted fixing! I wanted certain aspects of myself sorting out. However, as the counselling proceeded it became clear that if I could jettison the parts of me I found troublesome I would also lose parts of myself which I valued. We are complex realities and we need to learn to love what we are, both delightful and damaged, and put it all into the hands of the master potter to form into something unique and beautiful. Being a priest, as I am, can make things harder and should definitely have a health warning. People have such high expectations of us and we are so vulnerable, not least if we start to believe the sometimes totally unrealistic and absurd expectations of perfection which people put upon us. We should not be seduced to living up to these but rather put our effort into living down to the heart of ourselves, a heart trusting in God's love and mercy and not in our own efforts. Paul clearly knew about this way of being when he wrote, 'For when I am weak, then I am strong.'[6] Richard Rohr echoes the same theme, 'God takes me very seriously. But this frees me from the burden of having to do this chore myself.'[7]

The road to holiness is a long one. It takes more than a lifetime and struggling is inevitable as we live through loss, pain, thwarted desires (Reflection 2), accidents, joys, successes and failures (Reflection 6), but struggling put into the hands of God is constructive not destructive. (Reflection 1). Of course, we need God's grace and that is assured, but we also need the help and support of wise and compassionate friends (Reflection 5). So growing in holiness is not achieved by our effort or self-control; it is achieved through a gift of God to us and our humble and stumbling acceptance of it. This poem powerfully depicts the way to holiness:

> I have waged this war against myself for many
> years.
> It was terrible,
> but now I am disarmed.
> I am no longer frightened of anything
> because love banishes fear.
> I am disarmed of the need to be right
> and to justify myself by disqualifying others.
> I am no longer on the defensive,
> holding onto my riches.
> I just want to welcome and to share.

I don't hold onto my ideas and projects.
If someone shows me something better –
no, I shouldn't say better but good –
I accept them without regrets.
I no longer seek to compare.
What is good, true and real is always for me the best.
That is why I have no fear.
When we are disarmed and dispossessed of self,
when we open our hearts to the God-Man
who makes all things new
then he takes away past hurts
and reveals a new time
where everything is possible.[8]

This place 'where everything is possible' is indeed the place of holiness. It is the peace of discovering that we can be at home in ourselves and that God is and always has been at home there with us (Reflection 4). It is a coming home to what we have always dimly known was there, what we have glimpsed in holy others and what we have yearned for and struggled to achieve ourselves.

Reflection 1

Hiding from God

I was dozing off, in the centre of Oxford, sitting in the scorching heat, amongst the frenetic throng of shoppers, waiting for a friend to return before attending an ordination. Suddenly, I was brought back to consciousness by a voice saying, 'Do you know the Lord Jesus Christ?' My immediate thought was that it clearly wasn't aimed at me, but then with sinking heart I realised I was wearing a dog collar. I didn't open my eyes, hoping that the voice would move on, but it came again with even more insistence. 'Do you know the Lord Jesus Christ?' My immediately conceived answer, in the light of me clearly being ordained, was the facetious, 'Of course not, I'm an Anglican!' Before delivering this unhelpful quip, however, by the grace of God, I opened my eyes and saw sitting next to me an old, toothless, and very poor man. We fell into conversation and he told me that he had once 'known the Lord Jesus Christ' but had done 'bad things'. 'Well, that makes you and me both.' I replied. 'And I still do bad things. It seems to me that's how human beings are and that all we can really do is to ask for God's mercy and forgiveness.' My awaited friend returned, the ordination beckoned and we moved off.

That man, however, stayed in my prayers and I remembered him later when I was preparing a sermon on the healing of the ten lepers in Luke's gospel.[1] It seemed to me that his plea and mine, and indeed that of us all, needed to be the same as the lepers', 'Jesus, Master, have mercy on us!'[2] When Jesus saw the lepers and heard their cry, his response was immediate and clear: 'Go and show yourselves to the priests.'[3] This must have seemed a most confusing and hurtful directive since lepers were only required to show themselves to the priest when they were healed. Was he mocking them, this travelling preacher man? Nevertheless, helpless and hopeless as they were, with nothing to lose, they obeyed and were 'made clean'. When we cry for mercy, as the lepers did, a similar trust and obedience is asked of us, 'Go and show yourself,' not to the priest but to God. We are asked to go and bring ourselves into God's presence as we really are.

We are not many of us very willing to do this. We are not keen to show to God, others or ourselves the complex reality of what we are. Most of us, if we're lucky, have a few strong hands to play in life, to show others and to offer. We all basically enjoy playing these 'strong hands' because they show us off in the best possible light. Indeed, many of us will busily manipulate situations to give us the showcase that we need to use our best skills. I well remember arriving in my first parish as an arrogant new curate, rather proud of all the giftedness I thought I had to offer: able worker with young people; good preacher and teacher; a person of wide pastoral experience etc. Because of my determination to 'play one of my strong hands' it took me ages to see that God wanted me to work with the older people. I had no idea how to do this, and was, therefore, fearful that I might not be shown to good advantage. Actually, of course, once I started to work with them, listened to them and with them to God, I was able to find a much better way forward than if I had been relying on my giftedness alone. The need to play our 'strong hands' can be almost endemic amongst us and this is a great pity because it is not always from the places where we feel most confident, where we think we understand, that the deepest growth can occur. As Yehuda Amichai reflects,

From the place where we are right
flowers will never grow
in the spring.
The place where we are right
is hard and trampled
like a yard.
But doubt and loves
dig up the world
like a mole, a plough.
And a whisper will be heard in the place
where the ruined
house once stood.[4]

Of course, none of this is to deny that we must learn to

recognise our God-given gifts and to feel confident to use them. God, however, in my experience and in that of many of the people I have worked with, seems to be nowhere near as interested in our playing 'our strong cards' as we are! Indeed, if we concentrate too much on doing what we think we are good at it can make us arrogant, self-dependent and even intolerant of others who are less gifted. As Dag Hammarskjöld challenges us in his journal, *Markings*:

> 'Better than other people.' Sometimes he says: 'That, at least, you are.' But more often 'Why should you be? Either you are what you can be, or not – like other people.'[5]

Our capabilities are often an abstraction, at best a pattern rather than a fact, and the key thing to grasp is that we are capable of doing whatever God enables us to do. The enterprise is God's and how our capabilities play into that is in his hands, even to the extent that what might be asked of us is our willingness to be done to as much as to do, our willingness to be used or not used. I am always deeply moved by the Methodist Covenant Prayer although I find it almost impossible to pray:

> I am no longer my own but yours.
> Put me to what you will,
> rank me with whom you will;
> put me to doing,
>   put me to suffering;

> let me be employed for you
>   or laid aside for you
> exalted for you
>   or brought low for you;
> let me be full,
>   let me be empty,
> let me have all things,
>   let me have nothing;
> I freely and wholeheartedly yield all things
> to your pleasure and disposal.[6]

God wants us to offer him our strong and our weak 'hands' which can, of course, both in their different ways, make us struggle with holiness. What in fact we are invited to show God, to bring consciously into God's presence, is the totality of our being. Not just our giftedness but that which fills us with despair, shame, fear, panic, frustration and even disgust. Recently, through a succession of unlikely events, I found myself sitting, thinking and praying in my old undergraduate room at college. Sitting there made me very thoughtful. What exactly was the relationship between the young woman of then and the middle-aged woman of now? How were they connected? I could see growth but I also despaired that some essential key elements still troubled me and made me vulnerable. If we fail to offer these aspects of our reality to God he cannot work with them and our lives and ministries are impaired. In an article on prayer Jack Nicholls quotes Mother Mary Clare of the Sisters of the Love of God,

> When you go before God in prayer you cannot leave anything behind. You carry in your heart every person, every incident, every thought, every feeling you have ever had and as you lay yourself before God so you bring all the mess as well. 'My prayer', she said, 'is really one sentence: "Here I am, what a mess."'[7]

'Here I am, what a mess' is powerful indeed. In the early days of being a priest, I was always very tense when I celebrated the Eucharist. I was a curate in a church with a very formal liturgy and initially I struggled to do everything in the way to which the people there were accustomed. One day, my nervousness led me to spill the wine all over the altar cloth. I was horrified by the mess. The whole altar was covered in red. I was so upset but knew I must carry on and as I said the words of consecration it was borne in on me that God's intervention in the world through the death of Christ was much nearer to this mess I was witnessing than the very well-ordered celebration which we normally have; that the spilling of Christ's blood involved a handing over to the forces of chaos and destruction which was what we were celebrating in this act. That picture has been etched on my mind and as I celebrate communion now it powerfully reminds me of the risk and cost of God's action in Christ.

I used this quotation, 'Here I am, what a mess' in a Quiet Day for the ordinands at college along with what I considered to be a great richness of other thoughts and ideas! It was this thought, however, and this thought alone, which people mentioned to me again and again that term. Somehow it really resonated in their hearts. If we hide from the unacceptable parts of our lives and refuse to take them with us in prayer then God cannot work with us and gradually change us into his likeness. Mother Mary Clare's comment suggests that inevitably we cannot leave bits of ourselves behind when we pray but what we often do, of course, is fail to acknowledge the reality of this to ourselves.

I have lived much of my Christian life saying that God loves me but behaving as if I'm convinced he is out to get me: that if I really let him in on my world, he will do things to me which will hurt and harm me. Can I really believe what I both say and preach, that I am 'beloved of God', if I am determined to hide myself from God and unwilling to entrust my whole self to him? People think I am very open. 'What you see is what you get' is something I often hear said of me. Ha! It's true up to a point but there are deeply hidden depths which I am terrified to give up to anyone. Recently, I was sitting talking to a close friend late into the night with the comforting help of a bottle of red wine. She suddenly said, 'You know, you often come up to things I think you want to tell me and you don't. I just want to say that I notice and that I think it would be all right if you told me! But I want to stress there's absolutely no pressure to do so because I love you anyway.' I was shocked and taken aback! Was I so very transparent? If so, I didn't like the vulnerability that made me feel. I was not hiding things well enough. Yes I knew she loved me and I loved her but would she still love me if she *really* knew me? That was the agony. I was unsure and scuttled quickly off to bed. It troubled me though and I couldn't sleep. Obviously, I didn't really believe in her love if I couldn't trust her with myself. It was just a fair weather thing and no real use. So, the next morning I went for it and shared the issue which she had sensed I was withholding. I was terrified and felt sick. It felt very out of control to have it in the open. However, she was wonderful, gentle and accepting and now I feel so much better that she knows and hasn't turned away. I also realised what a block it had been to the deepening of our relationship and understanding. I explain this at length because I think it can inform our relationship with God. Our failure to believe enough in his love, to entrust the mess of our real selves to him, is a serious barrier to the joy of knowing him better.

This is a real challenge for us! We all struggle with learning to see who we are and to stop hiding from ourselves. One of the givens of living in community as we do in a theological college is that all of us, students and staff included, have a mirror lifted up to ourselves. I tell the ordinands that we will all do well to look in it! What is interesting is that people always suppose that what they will be shown in the 'mirror' of our community is their inadequacies and faults. This will sometimes be the case, but what is more often shown to us is that which others find delightful or helpful, the gifts in which they rejoice. These are often much harder for us to take on board than the negative things. I contrast this with an incident with my daughter Beth when she was tiny. I looked at her one day and told her what beautiful eyes she had. I have always remembered her response, 'Yes, Mummy, I know. Thank you.' This gave me real pause for thought as I realised how entirely beyond adults this straightforward response would be. How we have lost the ability to receive good things from each other.

One of the oddities I have found, again and again, in people as I have listened to them in a counselling capacity is their unwillingness to pray about the problems which they bring to me. One of my clients said very proudly to me recently, looking for my affirmation, 'Oh, I've prayed about it all now that I've got it sorted out!' Of course, I said I was pleased that after all the weeks we had been talking she had finally felt able to pray but I was still sad that it was the finished product rather than the 'mess' which she offered to God in prayer. So very often people in a mess (and that's most of us most of the time) feel they can't pray because they can't say the words that they think God wants to hear. We fear that we can only pray by giving God the right answers. In fact, the biggest danger is simply not to pray, to fail to be in conversation with the God who loves us. Far better to say to God, if it is your truth, that, for example, you want to stop desiring this person because you know it will hurt others and that you, at the same time, will die if you have to give the person up! Tell God that you really want to forgive this person for what they have done, but you also want to hate them forever! Trust God with the mess and inconsistency! The response God wants is the response we can make even if the stuff of our response is sometimes contradiction, confusion and irrationality. Invite him to be part of the resolution, to help you to begin to grow into the person whom he yearns for you to become. I am always helped in this by Jesus in the Garden of Gethsemane. He prayed as he felt. He longed that God would take the cup from him.[8] He asked God for what he wanted, inviting him into the mess, but none the less was able to say 'Yet not my will but yours be done.'[9] He was able, in these hugely terrifying circumstances, to trust himself absolutely to the God whom he knew loved him.

God doesn't want us to pretend. We don't need to protect him from the truth. As George Appleton's telling prayer says,

> O God, you desire truth in the innermost heart; forgive me my sins against truth; the untruth within me, the half-lies, the evasions, the exaggerations, the lying silences, the self-deceits, the masks I wear before the world. Let me stand naked before you, and see myself as I really am. Then, grant me truth in my inward parts and keep me in truth always.[10]

God can live with the reality that we are still sinners even if *we* find it hard to do so! The evangelical tradition in which I have my roots has a practice of asking people to offer testimonies about what God has done in their lives. I have always found this most disconcerting, not least because it makes me feel inadequate on every front! Firstly, people seem to have lived such terrible and rather exciting lives before they meet Jesus and sccondly, all now seems to be fine and they are sailing on into the sunset. I am left thinking that my testimony would have to be something like this: 'I was a sinner before I met Jesus (and probably not a very exciting one), then I met Jesus and sadly I'm still a sinner.' You see all the people of real faith that I know are sinners still, but now sinners on the way. What we all need to do is to learn to be more up front about it. I am reminded of a Peanuts cartoon which Mike Yaconelli cites in his book, *Messy Spirituality*.

> Charlie Brown comes to visit Lucy at her 5 cent psychiatrist booth. Lucy says to Charlie Brown that life is like a cruise liner. Some people put their deckchairs up at the back of the liner and like to look back to where they have come from. Others like to pitch their deckchair at the front and look ahead to where they are going. What about you, Charlie Brown? Where do you put your deckchair on the cruise liner of life? There is a long, sad, bemused pause. 'Heck,' Charlie Brown says, 'I don't even know how to put my deckchair up!'[11]

Believe you me, having listened in depth to the lives of many people, it seems to me this is the reality for most of us!

The challenge is to learn to pray as we are and this is closely linked to our ability to accept ourselves as we are and not as the idealised people we might imagine ourselves to be. We must come to accept that it is when our lives are in the biggest mess and when our desires are strongest and our minds most distracted that we can really begin to grow in our knowledge of ourselves as real people. This is exactly the point at which we must urgently and with most benefit offer ourselves to God in prayer.

The lepers showed themselves to the priest, and this act of considerable faith was honoured by their healing. We too need to take ourselves, every part of the complexity which is us, into God's presence, leaving nothing behind. Then our healing and growth is also possible. For one and one only of the lepers, the Samaritan, the foreigner, the outcast, did it lead to his offering thanks to God. They were certainly all cured but perhaps only this one was made whole as he alone understood that what he had received was a gift and gave thanks to God.

There is a beautiful church lying in a tiny hamlet, near an ancient ford by the River Trent. It was built by a fifthteenth-century wool merchant as a penance to save his soul. I have no idea what he did! This church makes me offer a wry smile. The builder, the very human and fallible John Barton, confusing the material and the spiritual, built the church one-sided. If you stand near the manor house the church looks ornate and decorated, if you stand and look from the farm labourers' cottages on the other side it looks plain as plain can be. This makes me think of me, and it makes me think of all of us. How often we behave just like John Barton. We show our good and respectable face to God, to others and even to ourselves. However, if we only allowed ourselves to peer round the corner, certainly not hidden from God and often not hidden from others or ourselves is the other side. Nobody is fooling anybody so why do we so often behave like this?

I believe that the reasons lie deep in our childhoods. When we are young we look into the faces of those around us to see who we are and how we are doing. Ideally, for our wellbeing, we need those eyes to reflect back to us unconditional love and acceptance. Unfortunately, this does not happen as none of us are surrounded by perfect people and it is all too easy to get things wrong. All those who care for us, however well, are only human and this inevitably means that they have needs themselves which have only been half met. So these guides are problematic for us. Firstly, they cannot love us unconditionally and secondly, as we interact with them we, in turn, can start to take upon ourselves their deficits, the things which they failed to be given. So basically the problem is that we are adrift in a world where nobody really has the faintest idea what it might feel like to be unconditionally loved. This is beyond our experience. Love, even the best we can offer, always comes with provisos and limitations.

Just how difficult it is to get this right as a parent was borne in on me early in my son James' life. At infant school, his closest friends were a delightful couple of identical twins. When they moved to a new school James was utterly bereft. At lunchtime he just stood by himself on the edge of the playground and watched the other lads playing football. He loved football and I was sure that if he could join in he would make some new friends, so I started to encourage him to play. One day on the way to school talking about playtime he said to me, 'Mummy, it's the rough boys who play football. I am not a rough boy.' Then he horrified me by adding with his seven-year-old's frankness, 'Is that a problem to you?' It made me realise how easy it is for misunderstanding to grow about what is hoped for and acceptable. Whether I wanted a boy who could play football or was rough was not the issue, but it was so easy for James to think that it was.

Because we tend to think about God in the way we think about each other, these difficulties we have about knowing ourselves unconditionally loved, are reflected in that relationship too. We find it very hard to believe that God loves us as we are, that he loves us unconditionally and accepts us unreservedly. We are always tempted to make God in our own image, indeed it is a great struggle not to. Gerard Hughes illustrates this in his excellent book *God of Surprises*,

> If our experience has taught us to think of God as a policeman type figure, whose predominant interest is in our faults, and if our encounters with him have been mostly in cold churches where we were bored out of our minds with barely audible services and sermons presenting God as he who disapproves of most of the things we like, then we are not likely to want to turn to him, no matter how many people may tell us that prayer is necessary.[12]

The task then is both intellectual and emotional. We may know intellectually that God is not like the policeman cited above but this does not help much if we still feel that he is. So our prayers for ourselves and others must be as much for a change in the way we *feel* about God as they are for the way we *think* about him. The more we come to believe in God as unconditionally loving, accepting and affirming the more we will be able to take the risk of showing him who we really are and of sharing with him the lives that we really live. As we begin to believe new things of God it will enable us to believe new things about ourselves. 'In love there is no room for fear; indeed perfect love banishes fear.'[13]

This journey of transformation and acceptance is beautifully explored by Trevor Dennis in his short story:

> The child was young enough to know that speaking to God was the most natural thing in all the world, to know that God laughed and cried, to know that God's house was not a grand place, but small and intimate, warm, comfortable and very safe, and that God had carpet slippers on her feet. She had not yet been taught to be afraid of God, or that she was not good enough for her, or that she always had to be on best behaviour with her and keep as many secrets from her as she could. She liked God and liked her company. It was as simple for her as that.
>
> But the child grew up, and learned she had to be more sophisticated. Adults told her it was much

more complicated. Adults spoke of guilt, confession and praise. Adults taught her to be polite with God, to doff her cap, bend the knee, touch her forelock and watch her step. Adults filled her silences with words to say and songs to sing, and those put God on such a high pedestal that she could not see her anymore, let alone reach to kiss her. In fact, God was no longer for kissing. Adults taught her that, too. They turned her God into a 'He' with a large capital 'H', removed His carpet slippers, and clothed Him with High Dignity.

For a long time the growing child, moved inexorably towards adulthood and then arriving there, believed what she was told. She learned that it was not proper to *like* God. She was to *love* God instead, so long as underneath she was secretly afraid.

Yet the memories of childhood, by the mercy of God, did not leave her entirely. Deep in her mind and soul they still talked softly, producing in her an unease, a holy doubt, a sense of something precious that was lost, and a longing to find it again.

One day she packed her spiritual bags and left. She left behind the people who were content to remain where they were. She left those who were sure they had arrived, and spoke as if they owned the Promised Land. She abandoned their terrifying certainties, and went out into what they told her was no-man's land, no-woman's land, no-god's land. She tried also, as far as she could, to leave behind those people's fear of God, the fear that lurked beneath their talk of love and praise. A new fear came upon her, the fear of the unknown, the fear of loneliness. She packed that in her bag, along with her unease, her yearning, her holy doubt, and a new sense of adventure and a large exhilaration.

She passed many on the road going in the opposite direction, to the patches of ground she had left behind, to the familiar pieces of territory where all was known and no surprises were to be had.

Yet soon she was not alone. Others came and joined her.

'Don't look so serious!' someone said. 'Can you play anything?'

'A musical instrument, do you mean?'

'Yes.'

'I don't think so.'

'That's a funny answer. Try this.' He put a hand inside his coat and produced a tuba.

'But I can't. I mean I've never … How do you blow? I can't read music.'

'Try.'

'But this is ridiculous!'

'Yes, it is. Try.'

She picked up the tuba, cradled it awkwardly in her arms, put it to her lips and blew. She produced a singularly rude noise, and her companions fell about laughing.

'Wonderful!' they cried. 'That'll do. Come on!'

'But I can't do it properly at all!'

'You will. Come on!'

Lugging along the tuba as best she could, she started off again with her companions. They were still laughing. She noticed most of them had musical instruments of one kind or another. One poor man was pushing a piano.

The tuba was very big, and very heavy.

'Some of you aren't carrying anything,' she complained.

'Yes we are,' they replied. 'Our voices.'

'You mean you're the choir?'

'Exactly. You're beginning to understand. We travel light. The adults taught you too well, back there. That's why you're having to drag that great thing along. But we haven't far to go now.'

At the top of the next hill, the ones in the front of the group suddenly stopped.

'Listen to that!' they said.

Beneath them stretched a wide plain, and in the middle of it was the God the woman had set out to find, the God of her childhood. She, her God, out there, in the middle of the plain, was playing a saxophone. Its sound made bright the air, soft, lilting, inviting, sensuous, ethereal, a single instrument weaving together the sounds of heaven and earth and in-between. The woman had never heard anything so wonderful in all her life, nor so beautiful.

She put her lips to the mouthpiece of the tuba. Without hesitation or restraint she began to play a love-song, soft, lilting, inviting, sensuous, ethereal. It filled the plain and wove itself together with the sound of the saxophone.

Her companions took up their own instruments. Slowly they played or sang their way down the long slope onto the plain and out to its centre. By the time they reached God their music had become a romp, enough to wake the angels in their beds. Eventually it subsided again, fell back to a gentle pianissimo, rocked heaven back to sleep, and then, miraculously, became a single thread. All the notes became as one, sound merged with sound and made a single beauty.

In the midst of them God put down her saxophone, listened for a spell, and began to dance.[14]

Reflection 2

Dealing with Our Desires

As the deer pants for the water,
So my soul longs after you.
You alone are my heart's desire
And I long to worship you.

You alone are my strength, my shield,
To you alone may my spirit yield.
You alone are my heart's desire
And I long to worship you.

You're my friend and you are my brother,
Even though you are a King.
I love you more than any other,
So much more than anything.[1]

This song, based on Psalm 42, is one I have often been invited to sing over the years. It always gives me great pause for thought and has many times brought me close to tears. 'You alone are my heart's desire,' I have *never* been able to sing this as my truth. 'I love you more than any other, So much more than anything.' This also has proved beyond me. Always so many other strong desires in me for people and for things jostle to keep God on the margins. Do I then stop singing this? I have decided that, although this may never be my actuality, I can sing it as my aspiration. For I have begun to understand that I long for this to be my truth. I yearn to discover God at the heart of my desire.

Telling people that I'm trying to write about desire always draws out a similar response to that of my hairdresser which was simply 'Oh!?' This is partly of course because we often tend in this culture to equate desire with sex. However, it is also because we instinctively understand that desire is holy ground, at least to the extent that it is deeply private and important to us. We know that to speak of our desires is to speak of things which are very personal to us, things which matter, things which will give a lot away. Someone said to me that it was like sharing our dreams. As Yeats says,

> I have spread my dreams under your feet;
> Tread softly because you tread on my dreams.[2]

For Christians, desires can often seem to us quite simply to be wrong, unless of course they blend in seamlessly with the song at the beginning. It is our need for privacy that makes us slow to speak of our desires. They take us into those tender, vulnerable parts of ourselves which hold all that is most precious and sometimes also that of which we are most deeply ashamed and afraid. But, if God is a God of deep desire who has put this capacity into our hearts, then this most human of emotions must not be ignored but listened to and understood. It is a vital key to knowing who we are. It is a vital key to understanding our deep innermost needs. Many people deny that they even have desires, not least because desires are demanding of response and responsibilities. We need to learn that desires can be trusted, that they can be safely heard in our day-to-day living. They are our most honest experiences of ourselves. A friend once wrote to me:

> Our desires are our deep communication. They are where I meet who I am. These voices are mine. They speak for me. They are the power of me. Only when I refuse me do they threaten to overpower.

A man was 'sent' to me by his wife and his vicar because they were all having problems with his desires! He had fallen in love with another woman, was having an affair and didn't want to stop. Understandably, in the circumstances, he didn't much want to talk to me, and I can recall several very awkward sessions full of protective body language and very little communication. I, being very human, became exasperated and said, 'For goodness' sake, we're not going to get anywhere like this. How will we ever know if you should go off with this woman or stay with your wife if you won't even talk to me?' Later he told me how this had been a turning point for him. He realised that he was being offered the freedom to explore his situation and that I was taking his desires seriously. Of course, once we started to get in touch with his desires they were very complex and much more so than the comparatively easy choice of 'wife or lover?' As we explored the truth of his deep desires, he was able to see more clearly for what he yearned. In his case he finally opted to stay in his marriage but could not have done this successfully without first coming to a gracious understanding of his own desires.

Desire fills us to bursting with energy and whether denied or accepted does not go away. So an important task for us is to look our desires in the face, so to speak, to follow them back to the beginning, to understand their substance. We need to pay close attention to that little phrase 'I want'. We need to mark it with a flashing light every time it comes into our minds. In the novel *Henderson, the Rain King* by Saul Bellow the hero goes crashing about in his life doing all sorts of damage. Gradually he comes to recognise that his life is driven by that little phrase 'I want' screaming in his head. What is it he wants? That's hard to know. He thinks he knows until he tries it and then the hunger returns. So he goes on being driven, consuming one thing after another, always helpless to still the cry 'I want!'[3]

It is dangerous and very difficult to try to keep someone away from what they strongly desire. Often we will circumvent all moderation, justifying to ourselves our right to have what we desire and often organising our whole lives around the need to get it. We see this in the parables of Jesus: the man who sold *all* he owned in order to buy a field in which there was hidden treasure; the merchant who sold *everything* to buy just the one pearl of great value.[4] I think of the man or woman who can justify all manner of neglect of their spouse because they are intent on pursuing their desired career; the man or woman who betrays their marriage and destroys their family because they desire to be with their lover; the politicians who can justify shortcuts and deceit because they desire to stay in power. Desire is powerful, overwhelming and often wonderful. It is difficult to tame but it delights us because it makes us feel capable of being fully alive. It energises us. As Carol Shields says of a middle-aged character struggling with life in her recent novel *Unless*:

> Some essence has deserted her. A bodily evaporation has left her with nothing but hard, direct questions aimed in the region of her chest, and no one would ever suspect that she might be capable of rising to the upper ether of desire, wanting, wishing.[5]

Feeling desire gives us a very powerful experience of ourselves. A sharp, deep look inwards. In his excellent book *Befriending Our Desires* Philip Sheldrake rightly says, 'Our desires imply a condition of incompleteness because they speak to us of what we are not, or do not have.'[6] We need to take the time to, as it were, look our desires fully in the face to understand what they are telling us both about ourselves and about the human condition. We need to follow them back to the beginning for they will guide us back to the things which are missing. They will show us for what we yearn. Wanting is neither to be despised nor simply to be indulged; rather it needs to be understood for what it is. So, if someone strongly desires success and status, we need to follow this back to its root where perhaps it will appear as a deep lack of confidence, in not being 'good enough' and perhaps ultimately in struggling to believe that they are loveable. If someone desires a person, perhaps following this back to its root it will reveal a lack of security, a lack of nurture, fear of being alone and perhaps ultimately the need to be loved. If a person desires material possessions, perhaps when this is followed back to its root it will tell us of insecurity, of low self-esteem, again of the need to be loved. Maybe all these examples are actually about the same things, about aloneness, the need for connection and our desire for unconditional love. If we keep paying attention to our desires rather than suppressing them, or simply indulging them, then we will begin to understand ourselves better. Understand that we are made in the image of a God who knows desire and who desires us! So we may find the courage to bring to God in prayer our passionate need to be desired and loved. That is the nub of the issue, for we will come to understand that this longing has been planted in us by the hand of God and that it is taking us towards him not away.

We are all created with this need to be loved and affirmed and we all expend a great deal of energy to get these needs met. I can remember once describing myself very unflatteringly as a white plastic coffee cup (you know the type) being filled up with people's love, affirmation, care and nurture. These are all things I desperately need and use much energy to run after. The problem, however, is that there is a crack in the bottom of the cup! So I feel great for a bit but then it all gradually drains away until I need it all over again. What we painfully learn is that people cannot entirely meet this need, that they will fail us and let us down. The scale of the task is beyond all of us. As Henri Nouwen says, 'There is a deep hole in your being like an abyss. You will never succeed in filling that hole, because your needs are inexhaustible.'[7]

So what are we to learn from the existence of this deep hole within us which our desires drive us to attempt to fill? At the heart of Christian spirituality, is the understanding that these deep longings can only ultimately be satisfied by God. It is as if our desires are infinite and cannot be settled by anything or anyone less. So if we rush to fill it with, for example, human love or success we simply dull the ache for a while until the cup drains out again. Can we believe that God is able to fulfil us beyond our wildest dreams? That our desire is simply the other half of his desire for us, the mirror image of the image in which we are made? Can we possibly begin to grasp that desire can only truly be met if it is mutual? So we need not to look outside ourselves to meet our need, to calm the 'I wants', but to look inward to the place where God can hold us and make us whole. As Augustine writes, 'You have made us for yourself, and our hearts are restless till they find rest in you.'[8]

In each of us there is a place which is properly God's, a space, at the heart of us, which it is not possible to fill with anything else. I am very fortunate to live in the wonderful city of Durham. Those who have visited will know that at the centre, dominating all else, is the Norman cathedral. I like to think of this as a huge space for God at the heart of our city. Of course, it is enclosed by a building of great physical beauty but primarily it is a place, a space in which to wonder at God and to worship him. A place in which to sit and be with God in a special way. That is its purpose. Every day on my way to work I go into the cathedral to delight in this space. I only wish I was half as assiduous at visiting the sacred space in myself. For, of course, there is in each of us the same space with the same purpose and I suspect in God's eyes surrounded by a being with more beauty and importance to him even than Durham Cathedral!

So how do we respond to our desires so that they can help us to grow in holiness? We must begin by attending to the fact that God desires us. Probably our deepest desire is to be desired and if we are lucky we know in human terms what it feels like. It certainly doesn't leave us unchanged even if the desiring is not welcome! Desire gets through to us, we know when it's there, and it affects us and our behaviour. So if God does desire us it must have an even more profound influence on our lives.

The notion that God desires us is difficult for most of us to get our heads around. In as much as we can embrace this idea most of us would probably like God's desire to be tidy and restrained. It comes then as something of a shock to encounter the Song of Songs in the Old Testament. This book is often read as an allegory of God's love for his people but is essentially a book about just how badly two people want each other. There are long passages extolling the delights of the lover's body, heart-wrenching descriptions of just what these deep longings feel like and some imagining about when they will finally make love. In a recent sermon on this book the preacher said, 'This is about married love … or it should be!' I disagree. To me this book has all the marks of besotted 'in loveness'. The delightful preoccupation with the other which is almost a kind of madness. When we are 'sick' with love, when we cannot sleep, cannot eat, cannot think about anyone else. What C. S. Lewis calls, and I for one agree with him, the 'king of pleasures'.[9] It is soaring, transcendent, ready for self-sacrifice. Such 'in loveness' inspires us to become altruistic; personal happiness is irrelevant. All that matters is the good of the beloved. For once we can blur the edges of our selfhood and not be alone. It has such God-like characteristics but sadly for us, human 'in loveness' is flawed. We are unable to deliver what is promised, for it is notoriously fickle and transient.

Why then use this kind of love to describe God's love for us? Wouldn't the faithful, practical, day-to-day commitment of married love be better than this messy 'in loveness'? It seems that we need to learn to live with the idea of God as our lover in this deeply passionate connected way. Human 'in loveness' gives us a glimpse of what God's desire for us is like, its overwhelming intensity and delight. It also throws a challenging light on what loving 'God with all your heart, and with all your soul, with all your strength, and with all your mind'[10] might mean.

All other desires will find their right place if they are contained within God's desire for us and ours for him. This mutuality is what the psalmists so often discovered,

> You have said, 'Seek my face.'
> My heart says to you,
> 'Your face, Lord, do I seek.'[11]

Jesus of course also knew this mutuality. At his baptism God said, 'You are my beloved Son; in you I delight.'[12] Jesus is loved, affirmed and desired by God. Unsurprisingly, in that he was truly human, immediately after this affirmation, he was tempted to fill God's holy space in him by running after other desires: food, power and wealth. However, the root of Jesus' identity was both in knowing himself desired by God and in his full response to that desire. It was this that enabled him to follow through the decisions which his life and death entailed. These were such hard decisions that they could only have been possible within his certainty of God's love and his trust in the goodness of God's desire for him.

Sadly, we can only partially know the nature of God's

desire for us and will only ever be able to respond inadequately. None the less, the choice is before us, whether to run with the world's dreams or to gamble on God, to trust that we will indeed find our fulfilment and happiness, our own authentic dream, in God's dreams and desires for each of us. If we are to do so we will need to resist the seductive voices that lure us with the possibility that our insatiable desire can be fulfilled in any other way.

Of course, we do receive many intimations of God through the mediation of other people and learning how to desire them in the right way is a crucial step forward; our desire must cease, for example, to be one of ownership or of overwhelming need. God's love embraces rather than excludes the best in all our human experiences of loving. So we are not asked by God to discount other forms of love, for they teach us much, but we are not to mistake them for what they are not. Whilst they can give us an inkling of the nature of love, they are not the fulfilment in God which is the only way of ultimately meeting our human longing. Desire always calls us on to what is beyond ourselves and draws us to a lifetime of becoming. Our relationship with God must necessarily always be developing and deepening. God is always calling us on. As R. S. Thomas reminds us in his poem 'Pilgrimages':

> He is such a fast God,
> Always before us and
> Leaving as we arrive.[13]

Reflection 3

The Gifts of Forgiveness

Everything had fallen apart. A ministry which had started with such commitment to serving God and with the enthusiastic support of friends and family was in tatters. Too many times in my job have I needed to sit with clergy in the ruins of their life and ministry … sometimes it was drink, sometimes it was fraud, sometimes it was an affair, sometimes it was mental illness, sometimes it was struggles with sexuality. The underlying reasons so deeply complex, and the outcome so catastrophic. I always found such times unbearably sad and my heart was filled with compassion for the clergy themselves and for all the many others who inevitably get caught up and hurt in such a maelstrom. A hard situation but made so much harder by the press laying siege to the house, desperate for 'the story'. Such good fodder for the Sunday newspapers! What rewarding news it seems to be when someone has been unable to live up to their promises and our expectations. How the mighty are fallen! What satisfaction people seem to take in knowing that clergy too have feet of clay.

This kind of self-righteous baying for blood is exactly the situation in which Jesus found himself.[1] What was he writing in the dust? We will never know but we do know that it had the effect of gaining Jesus the control of an incredibly difficult and dangerous situation. The woman had been thrust before him, being used as a thing, a means of focusing the escalating dispute between Jesus and the Pharisees. She had been caught in the act of adultery and we can only attempt to imagine the state she was in: publicly humiliated and terrified that she would be stoned to death. Most of us presented with a pastoral crisis like this would burst into ill-considered speech and action. Not so Jesus: he was thoughtfully silent as he drew in the dust. This calmed things down, stopped the spiral towards tragedy and enabled him to take control, enraging the Pharisees who kept provoking him with more questions. He created a space in time which allowed their anger to calm down, a space in which he could take stock, perhaps deal with his own fears and uncertainties, maybe suppress his own anger at this outrage and pray to his Father. His action created the possibility of silence, the kind of silence in which God can be heard and finally from this space emerged the well-considered response, 'Let whichever of you is free from sin throw the first stone at her.'[2]

The effect of this was immediate and amazing. The men started to slink away, the most important and influential first, leaving just the two of them standing there: a sinful frightened woman and the Son of God, the only one who could fulfil the requirement. Jesus was able to condemn her, the only one able to throw the first stone, but he chose not to do so. Instead he asked her, 'Where are they? Has no one condemned you?' First he established the fact that no human religious authority claimed the right to act as judge, though they had certainly seemed keen enough earlier, then he claimed the right for himself. 'Neither do I condemn you. Go; do not sin again.'

So she escaped condemnation and was free to regain her life. Crises are always opportunities for reanalysis and change and this woman had certainly been through some major crises in only a very short time. She had been caught committing adultery, publicly humiliated, terrified, scorned, faced possible death, met Jesus and then been let off. She had her life returned to her. What would she do with this gift?

All of us face crises at times and all of us do things which are wrong, but the extraordinary truth is for us, as it was for this woman, that the only person qualified to throw the stone chooses not to. Why is this? Why does God choose to forgive us rather than condemn us? Because he loves us and chooses above all to stay in relationship with us. Of course, the way we behave often hurts God but, rather than making us pay for it, he chooses to take this within himself, containing the pain of it so that, whatever the cost, he can keep in relationship with us. Through forgiveness he also yearns 'to turn an evil act into an occasion of greater good.'[3] So as he contains the sins of this woman, it is to give her life.

Many years ago I recall listening to a Malcolm Muggeridge TV programme in which he said significantly, 'The only thing we take out of this life with us is our soul. So what happens to us only ultimately matters for what it has done to shape our souls.' So the question for this woman is, having her life restored to her, what will this incident have done to her soul? Will she have gained in understanding or changed? Will she have grown in holiness?

The importance of forgiveness is that it releases us from the past, into our present and offers us the possibility of a different future. As Desmond Tutu put it, 'True forgiveness deals with the past, all of the past, to make the future possible.'[4] This was his determination about the Truth Commission, that South Africa would have a future; because through this process of confession, absolution and reconciliation, a future free from the past would be possible. Without this process South Africa would have been shackled forever by the outrage of apartheid.

As an Anglican priest, I have become increasingly moved and influenced by the words of the prayer of absolution.

> Almighty God,
> Who forgives all those who truly repent,
> Have mercy upon you,
> Pardon and deliver you from all your sins,
> Confirm and strengthen you in all goodness,
> And keep you in life eternal;

Through Jesus Christ our Lord.
Amen[5]

I have always seen this as declaring the forgiveness of sins and that is, of course, its nature. However, I have increasingly come to see that it is most importantly about growing in holiness. That God forgives our sins, in order that we can be 'confirmed and strengthened in all goodness'. That whatever little seed of goodness we have, whatever the woman was able to gain from all her mistakes and experiences, is God's desired outcome from the forgiveness. Forgiveness is about securing a future orientation; that is what is important to God. We are freed from the consequences of our sin in order to grow, to go forward, to be confirmed and strengthened in whatever goodness we have and to stay in close loving relationship with the God who is our teacher in this. That is God's project of forgiveness with us.

What constantly amazes me is the extent to which we will go to circumvent this project of God's. I am astonished by the huge problems we have both with giving and receiving forgiveness. Most of us just don't attend to it. I often use in my lectures the image of each of us having a big box in our lives with a hinged top. When things go wrong we simply stuff them in the box, close the lid and sit on it. Over a lifetime this can cause a whole range of problems. Typically people come for help in middle age. What they are experiencing are the effects of a full box! It's taking them all their time and energy to keep the lid shut and even then things still creep out around the edges. In his excellent book *Crossing* Mark Barrett explores this by referring to Anthony Minghella's film *The Talented Mr Ripley*,

> Tom Ripley explains how he deals with the psychological weight of being a murderer. 'Don't you put the past in a room, in the cellar, and lock the door and just never go in there? Because that's what I do,' he tells us. 'Then you meet someone special and all you want to do is toss them the key and say open up, step inside, but you can't because it's dark and there are demons and if anyone saw how ugly it was …'
>
> I realised that, like Minghella's character, I had gone through life putting into a deep, dark room the emotions and experiences, the aspects of myself, I didn't want to deal with. I too was adept at closing the door and walking away. Perhaps the contents of my basement were less lurid than those of Ripley: nevertheless the spiritual and emotional lost property does not sit quietly. It has a way of rising up again, cluttering our tidy hallways at the moments we least expect it.[6]

So some people have problems because they refuse to look, and other people can have problems because they keep looking in the box. They routinely refer to it in order to, for example, refuel anger, resentment or guilt. This of course binds them to the past. What is necessary in either case is a good clear out; but what is far better is that things are dealt with as we go along and that nothing is left to accumulate in the box. Forgiveness is a creative act which opens up a new future, as Clarissa Pinkola Estes says about forgiveness in *Women Who Run With the Wolves*:

> There is no lariat snare around your ankle stretching from way back there to here. You are free to go. It may not have turned out to be happily ever after, but most certainly there is now a fresh once upon a time waiting for you from this day forward.[7]

In my experience of working with people on forgiveness, one of the biggest obstacles which people often have is that forgiving might imply that the offence does not matter. That the person will simply 'get away with it'. I would be rich indeed if I had a tenner for everyone who has said that to me in counselling sessions. C. S. Lewis is helpful on this:

> There is all the difference in the world between forgiving and excusing. Forgiveness says: 'Yes you have done this thing, but I accept your apology, I will never hold it against you …' But excusing says: 'I see that you couldn't help it, or didn't mean it, you weren't really to blame.' If one was not really to blame then there is nothing to forgive. In that sense forgiveness and excusing are almost opposites.[8]

Before forgiveness is offered, before the injured person decides to 'contain the sting and outrage of it'[9] themselves, the offences need to be fully revealed and judged.

It must be very clear to what a person is giving up their right. This is often a problem in Christian circles. I think of people I have counselled who have been badly abused by a parent. As Christians they know they should forgive, as human beings they know they need to be freed to move on. All too often though, they make excuses for the offender, 'It was hard for him. He didn't really know what he was doing. He wasn't to blame.' This approach really does not help. The person must stand charged first; then and only then can forgiveness be offered. Such forgiveness is not cheap, easy and unimportant. We must always remember that it cost Jesus everything on the cross. As Dag Hammarskjöld reflected in *Markings*, 'Forgiveness breaks the chains of causality, because he who forgives you – out of love – takes upon himself the consequences of what you have done. Forgiveness, therefore, always entails sacrifice.'[10]

I think of a woman I have talked with who had an abortion. As I listened to her story it was obvious to me that she had been in a very complex situation and I thoroughly understood the reasons why she had taken this decision. She, however, felt very guilty and knew she wanted to own before God her failure and weakness in the situation. She needed to be clear what she was asking God to forgive. She felt that she had harmed the other and had harmed the other in herself. Eventually, she offered this symbolically, placing her confession on the altar during a Eucharist. We are incapable of hearing God's word of forgiveness if we have not turned to our past, owned it and offered it to God and sometimes we are asked to make that journey with another. If we delude ourselves and fail to face things it makes the possibility of forgiveness very difficult.

A person in the Bible who had considerable problems with forgiveness was the unmerciful servant in Matthew 18.[11] Was he really so evil that having his own debts cancelled he could not be merciful to others? Perhaps, but it seems possible to me that the problem might have been more about a lack of surety than a lack of generosity. I don't think he really believed in his master's gift. I think that he was terrified that his master would change his mind and call in his debts after all, so he set off to get as much of the money owing to him as he could … just in case! We sometimes behave like this. Surely, if we really believe ourselves to be unreservedly forgiven by God we will not find it hard to forgive others. But do we really believe it? That's the problem. Clearly, the servant had never properly encountered his master for he did not know his real nature.

'I know that God forgives people who are truly sorry but I could never forgive myself for what I have done.' I quite often hear this kind of thing as a counsellor and, if I'm honest, it really irritates me. For such a statement reveals some huge misunderstandings about God and his love for us. I want to say, 'If God has forgiven you what possible right have you not to forgive yourself?' If God deeply loves us and desires us surely it is simply crazy to think that it is right for us to hate ourselves and to withhold the forgiveness which God so freely offers. 'Love your neighbour as yourself,'[12] we are taught by Jesus. We are to forgive others as we know ourselves to be forgiven. We are to love ourselves with the same passion as God loves us and that certainly means offering to ourselves the same generosity of spirit as we are called to have for others.

There is also in this parable a very clear connection between receiving forgiveness and offering it. We need to respond to forgiveness by offering forgiveness. 'Forgive us our sins as we forgive those who have sinned against us.'[13] The two stand or fall together. We cannot find the strength to offer forgiveness if we do not receive it ourselves. Neither can we receive it if we are unwilling to offer it. This is often the stumbling block in pastoral situations. I can think of many times when the so-called 'innocent party' withholds forgiveness, so that they don't have to find the humility to accept that they were wrong in any way, or that perhaps they will need themselves to be forgiven in turn. This withholding traps people, preventing the forward movement which is necessary for healing and it very often also traps those around them.

It must also be acknowledged that, for some, they see gains in withholding forgiveness. I recall the brother and sister who fell out many years ago over a seemingly trivial matter and whose hatred and anger have now become the energy which fuels their lives. Forgiveness would entail giving this up, which sadly they refuse to do. This affects their lives but more seriously the lives of their children and their grandchildren. It is definitely in this way that the children are punished for the sins of the parents.[14] I can think of a person who doggedly withholds forgiveness, even though he knows very well the level of genuine repentance of the other person. What does he gain? The pleasure of refusing to set her free? The power he perceives that his refusal gives him? What can be done if someone refuses to give or receive forgiveness? Is this woman always to be at the mercy of this man, to be trapped in this situation for ever? Sometimes the trapping occurs because the 'offender' is impossible to track down or is dead. This is particularly true in some abuse situations where people can wake up late to the reality of what has happened to them or what they have done. I am reminded of a question asked on the TV news by those who had lost loved ones through the massacres in Rwanda, 'How can we forgive if no one will admit to having done wrong?'[15] What about the many situations in which there seems to be no possibility of closure? Here we must make a clear distinction between forgiveness and reconciliation. In short, forgiveness takes one person; reconciliation takes two. We can, with God's help, let the offence go, whether as perpetrator or victim, and so move on into a future unencumbered by the past.

Of course, it is wonderful to also be reconciled but sadly this is not always possible. I counselled someone who had been abused by a vicar as a young woman. It had taken her ages to see that what had happened to her was not her fault and that she had suffered a huge abuse of trust and power. We gradually worked through the situation and she decided that she would like to go and speak with this priest. She wanted to make it clear to him how much he had damaged her, not just then but in all her subsequent life, in the hope that he would never harm anyone else in the same way. She had even rung up to arrange the meeting, when he died. So reconciliation was not possible, although, of course, it may never have been possible because we don't know how he would have reacted to what she had to say. Having been totally floored by this turn of events she finally decided to go and have the conversation with him by his grave. By offering her forgiveness to him in this way she was free to move on.

Our main problem with all of this is our inability to think with the mind and generosity of God. We all too often see forgiveness as a kind of transaction: sinner repents, makes restitution and is therefore forgiven. What is actually the case is that we are transferred into a different world altogether, the Kingdom of God, which wreaks havoc with our notion of fair play. The law of 'just deserts' is irrelevant here; rather we are dealing with a hugely generous outburst of love. We constantly struggle with God's complete otherness. I am reminded with a wry smile of the Parable of the Workers in the Vineyard,[16] of the outrage at the unfairness of the payments, an outrage and annoyance we know all too well that we would have shared. But this is the internal working of the Kingdom of God which we are told turns our world upside down. 'So the last will be first, and the first last.'[17]

We just do not get it, do we? And we won't get it until we are sufficiently at home in the Kingdom of God for it to be within our comprehension and experience – for things to come properly into focus. The truth is, though we cannot see it, that we live and breathe and have our being in a natural environment of forgiveness; like sea creatures in the sea. Every second we are held in God's forgiveness, whether we know it or not, and mostly we don't. If it were not so the world would fall apart. If justice were to be done, as we think it should be, all the world would fragment.

What we are dealing with here is a God whose nature it is almost impossible for us to grasp. The reconciliation he seeks with us has nothing of the premeditation of a transaction but has everything of the risk and undeserved spontaneity of an embrace! God loves us, and with those we love we are slow to judge, slow to anger and quick to allow the possibility of reconciliation. We fail to grasp the nature of forgiveness because we have such a pitifully weak grasp of the extent to which we are beloved of God. God is for ever reaching out to us and waiting upon the response. We all too easily see God through the eyes of our own lack of graciousness.

I am reminded of one of my favourite gospel stories.[18] The disciples who, just after Jesus has fed 4000 people with 7 loaves, find themselves in a boat with no bread, are oddly, in the light of recent events, very rattled by this. Jesus too seems understandably quite frustrated by their lack of comprehension and trust and starts asking them questions. 'When I broke 5 loaves for 5000 people how many baskets of leftovers were there? And when I broke 7 loaves for 4000 people how many baskets of leftovers were there?' The answers were 12 and 7 respectively. The disciples were confused, the mathematics presumably beyond them! Jesus is exasperated. 'And you still don't understand?' he asks. Generally, when you feed so many people with so little is there anything left over? No! So in simple terms there is loads left over. That's the point says Jesus and here you are arguing about who has forgotten the bread! You simply cannot understand the huge, unstinting generosity of your heavenly Father, can you? It is quite beyond your experience, this great extravagance of love.

Jesus, when faced with a close friend Peter, who had deeply let him down, did not go into an in-depth analysis of the failure, the reasons why, the depth of his repentance, how he would make amends, whether he deserved forgiveness. Instead he asked him one simple, and for Peter I am sure absolutely excruciating, question, 'Do you love me?' 'Yes Lord, you know that I love you.'[19] This was all that was required and, fortunately for us, our stumbling love of God is, like Peter's, enough – enough for 'the self-giving God'[20] to blow our sins away like a dandelion clock and stay in relationship with us.

> It is hard for anyone who makes a principle of avoiding pain or reactively paying it back on someone else to understand what forgiveness means, and aggressively independent natures cannot conceive of the miracle whereby one who pardons an injury contains the sting and outrage of it in the hope of preserving the relationship at any cost and turning an evil act into an occasion of greater good. Yet that is what the self-giving God has always done ... [21]

Reflection 4

Paying Attention

We collided in the market place, the three-year-old girl and I. She was giving all her attention to a beautiful, large multi-coloured ball in a string bag which she was spinning around and around and which she was watching with rapt concentration. I was rushing to meet someone for lunch, my attention not at all on the little girl and her ball, but on this partly written book, on what I needed to buy for tea and what I wanted to discuss over lunch. We collided for completely different reasons but both were related to the giving of attention: I because my attention was not in that place or moment at all and she because she was so completely absorbed in giving attention to her beautiful, new ball. Let us consider her attention issues first.

As a parish priest I found that doing infant school assemblies always did me a power of good even when they went astray, which they all too easily did! One day my colleague asked the children the question, 'Where are you?' Hands shot up all across the hall, 'School, Church

Street, Durham.' Still the required answer had not been given so the children exerted themselves further, 'England. Europe. The World.' Finally defeated, they looked to my colleague, who told them that they were in today, not yesterday or tomorrow but today! He then proceeded to deliver a short talk on the importance of living in the present. To conclude he said, 'Well, children, so where are we?' I groaned inwardly fearing what the answer would be. Loads of hands shot up, 'Durham' they said happily and completely oblivious of my colleague's efforts. The talk was good but missed its target because living in the present wasn't an issue for them. Very little children seem to have a special uncluttered way of being and, as the little girl with her ball showed us, they are totally absorbed in the present. Little children are the natural contemplatives. Sadly, the rest of us have to constantly relearn this attitude. We do not easily retain the ability to give our undivided attention to the present moment, to see what delight and intricacy there are in ordinary things. As Rainer Maria Rilke says, 'We gradually lose the eye for these riches, while children … quickly notice and love with their whole heart.'[1]

Under certain extreme circumstances adults can relearn the art of seeing. Brian Keenan in *An Evil Cradling*, the account of his five-year captivity as a hostage in Beirut, writes powerfully of his experience of being given a bowl of fruit in which there were some oranges. As he sees, feels, licks and smells the oranges, as he attends to them with all of his deprived senses, he has a deeply spiritual experience. He encounters oranges as he has never done before: 'The colour orange, the colour, the colour, my God the colour orange … Such wonder, such absolute wonder in such insignificant fruit.'[2] He determines not to eat the fruit, choosing instead to make it the focus of his attention, and as he does he is filled with both joy and love.

It is pertinent that both this quotation and that from Rilke tie together the giving of real attention and the perception that this brings with it a response of love and joy. It is as if, when we can really give attention to look, hear, touch and smell we can start to penetrate to the heart of the matter, and there we will find God. Is that why I never feel closer to the heart of God than when I am amongst young children, the most free dispensers of love and joy?

Paul reminds us in his letter to the Romans[3] that creation makes plain to us God's invisible qualities and as we give them real attention, they properly call forth delight, love and gratitude. We are overwhelmed with extraordinary gifts, but so often have lost the capacity to wonder and to offer our appreciation for what exists. Shug, a blues singer in the book *The Color Purple* shows a deep understanding of the extent to which God showers us with things to enjoy:

> God love everything you love … But more than anything else God love admiration.
>
> You saying God vain? I ast.
>
> Naw she say. Not vain, just wanting to share a good thing. I think it pisses God off if you walk by

> the color purple in a field somewhere and don't notice it.
>
> What he do when he pissed off? I ast.
>
> Oh, he makes something else. People think pleasing God is all God care about. But any fool living in the world can see he's always trying to please us back.[4]

So what were my attention issues as exhibited in the collision over the child's ball? Clearly, I was physically there but my attention was not. I was unable to stop the rush of my life and to focus in the present.

Most adults have long ago lost the ability to delight in the colours of a ball as it twizzles in its bag in just the same way as we have lost the ability to delight in a buttercup, someone's accent, the smell of good cooking, the sound of bird song, an autumn leaf, a broad grin. Grown-up people with all our responsibilities and cares, all our aspirations and fears, ceaselessly busy, fail to see what children can see and love. We find it very hard to be present, and live in the present. We are physically there but our hearts and minds are elsewhere.

My son has just started to drive and last week I took him out for the first time. This was, to say the least, a slightly hair-raising experience, leading to several rows as to *exactly* how fast he was going. It was very scary at times, but I can assure you that nothing would have induced me to get into that car if I hadn't been confident of one thing: that he could stop! The same applies to us in our daily life as to cars, for attention and stopping are inextricably bound up together. Unless we can stop, we will never hear God and grow in holiness. Neither do we stand the slightest chance either, individually or corporately, of living lives which are honouring to the Lord whom we try to serve.

The importance of stopping is obvious, not least because we make so many mistakes through our failure to stop: the wrong judgement; the inability to hear exactly what is being said; the failure to respond appropriately; the harsh word or put down; the neglect and the badly performed; the reacting rather than responding. What then pushes us on to live so badly? What is the pay-off? Donald Nicholl in his excellent book on holiness challenges us with this answer,

> In one word it is greed. Greed may take many forms. Often, of course, it takes the simple form of greed for food, or for sexual satisfaction; on other occasions it is greed for experience, whether of travel or of music or of culture in general; sometimes it takes the form of greed for information or, equally often, for flattery. But whatever form it takes greed generates hurry by leading us to try to push in more than there is really room for.[5]

It can also, of course, be about greed for success, status or affirmation or about being driven by, for example, fear, inadequacy, and lack of self-esteem. Usually, whatever the driving force, we find that we are no longer in charge of our lives when we fail to stop. I recall the senior churchman who told me how, having worked a very long day arrived back home at 11.30 in the evening and, listening to his answerphone, he started to work again. He realised then, that his working life, despite being full of worthwhile things, was out of control, that he'd lost the 'off button' if you like, or at least lost the capacity to operate it! Realising that we are living our lives badly because we are always, whatever we are doing, permanently distracted and, therefore, unable to give proper attention, is an important starting point.

We have already considered how we can all too easily progress through the world failing to give proper attention to creation and therefore failing to be moved by the wonder of it all. Part of the wonder of creation is other people and they are all too often a casualty of our inability to stop and pay attention. Paying proper attention to someone you are in love with is the easy end of the spectrum. Many an hour can be whiled away in such company intrigued by the person's former life, their views on issues or simply the sound of their voice, the feel of their skin and the beauty of their eyes. Total concentration on the other is easy and full of delight. However, paying full attention to most people is really hard work. Not everything to which we have to listen is riveting and much is repetition of what we have heard before. I am always amazed by how quickly someone senses that they are not being properly listened to and how quickly I know it when it happens to me. It can be very crushing to have a conversation where neither of you are fully present, but it all too often happens.

Giving the gift of attention to someone though is often transformatory for us. I confess to inwardly groaning sometimes as a new client comes to see me. The thought of the many hours which we will spend in each other's company over the coming months can initially fill me with despair. However, without fail, as they share with me the reality of their lives, I come to love them, not because I am a spectacularly loving person (far from it!) but because the process of giving attention to people, people whom you believe to be made in the image of God and therefore to be loveable, enables you to come to love them. It enables you also to respect them and always of course to learn from them. Many a time, to my shame, I have started off being critical and judgemental of a person; however, as I have offered the gift of my attention to them, I have come to respect and admire them and to understand that they, in their particular circumstances, have made a far better job of their life than I in the same circumstances could have made.

One of my favourite stories is 'We are Three' by Anthony de Mello. It teaches us many things, but certainly warns us of the danger and arrogance of failing to offer proper attention and respect. The danger too, of the quick judgement and the way in which this can blind us to the possibilities of what we can learn from each other.

> When the bishop's ship stopped at a remote island for a day, he determined to use the time as profitably as possible. He strolled along the sea shore and came across three fishermen mending their

nets. In Pidgin English they explained to him that centuries before they had been Christianized by missionaries. 'We, Christians!' they said, proudly pointing to one another.

The bishop was impressed. Did they know the Lord's Prayer? They had never heard of it. The bishop was shocked.

'What do you say, then, when you pray?'

'We lift eyes in heaven. We pray, "We are three, you are three, have mercy on us."'

The bishop was appalled at the primitive, the downright heretical nature of their prayer. So he spent the whole day teaching them the Lord's Prayer. The fishermen were poor learners, but they gave it all they had and before the bishop sailed away the next day he had the satisfaction of hearing them go through the whole formula without fault.

Months later the bishop's ship happened to pass by those islands again and the bishop, as he paced the deck saying his evening prayers, recalled with pleasure the three men on that distant island who were now able to pray, thanks to his patient efforts. While he was lost in thought he happened to look up and noticed a spot of light in the east. The light kept approaching the ship and, as the bishop gazed in wonder, he saw three figures walking on the water. The captain stopped the boat and everyone leaned over the rails to see this sight.

When they were within speaking distance, the

bishop recognised his three friends, the fishermen.

'Bishop!' they exclaimed. 'We hear your boat go past island and come hurry hurry to meet you.'

'What is it you want?' asked the awe-stricken bishop.

'Bishop,' they said, 'we so, so sorry. We forget lovely prayer. We say, "Our father in heaven, holy be your name, your kingdom come ...", then we forget. Please tell us prayer again.'

The bishop felt humbled.

'Go back to your home, my friends,' he said, 'and each time you pray, say, "We are three, you are three, have mercy on us!"[6]

Giving attention to another takes time and can often be hard work. It is not easy to search for the real self in the other but when you find it, it is like finding gold. You are meeting a unique other, beloved of God and totally irreplaceable in the scheme of things. In his moving and honest journal, *Part of a Journey*, Philip Toynbee says:

> To be fully extended according to one's own nature and capacities – that is the only thing that matters. And the beauty of it is that since every human soul is unique the light that it sees and the light that shines have never been seen or shone before.[7]

You are encountering through your giving of attention an otherness which you will find nowhere else and from which you are capable of gaining things which only that other can give to you. I count it as one of the most profound privileges in life to be offered the essence of another human being.

There are any number of things which can hijack our capacity to give attention to someone else: boredom, hunger, a bad back, tiredness, an itchy nose, frustration, being unable to see the time, to name but a few! The biggest block, however, is, most certainly, internal: our instinct to be distracted back to our own issues by what we hear, our ability to be angry with the other because we are really angry with ourselves, our inability to tolerate something in the other because we cannot tolerate it in ourselves. Alan McGlashan says, 'The secret is this: to grow quiet and listen.'[8] I say, 'The fear is this: what will we hear, if we grow quiet and listen?' We don't want to be exposed and for most of our lives we hide behind, for example: the job we do; the people we're with; the tasks we attempt; escapism into TV, videos, books. Anything in fact to avoid the stark reality of how and who we really are. We package ourselves to others and even to ourselves so that we will feel acceptable. Our resistance to the truth is immense. It is always a tense moment when as a counsellor you have to challenge a person's story of their 'truth'. It is very painful indeed to have to face up to having our carefully edited and packaged version of our identity and our life challenged. We can feel vulnerable, alone and overwhelmed as we face up to our weakness, our complex motivations, our fears, our resentments and anger, our neediness, our confusion and helplessness.

There is no doubt that we cannot pay proper attention to another if it is our custom to ignore our deep inner self. We need to begin where we are; to give proper attention to ourselves. As Jesus says, 'Love your neighbour as yourself.'[9] We cannot love our neighbour if we do not love ourselves first. Our honest and loving acceptance of all that we are will help us to accept the other. Our knowledge that we are beloved of God and unreservedly forgiven will allow us to extend the same generosity to the other. Our belief in our unique importance to God will help us to offer appropriate respect to the other.

Giving attention is an aspect of giving love and what we seek to offer to ourselves and others should properly be something which we seek to offer to God. Indeed, our ability to ever offer real attention in any context is closely linked to our ability to offer real attention to God. Iris Murdoch writes that, 'Prayer is properly not petition, but an attention to God which is a form of love.'[10]

Giving our attention to God sounds easy but, as we all know, it frequently defeats us. As an opinionated teenager at Taizé many years ago, I remember telling one of the brothers how impressed I was by his willingness to worship so many times a day. He bluntly disabused me of my admiration by telling me that very often all he could offer was his willingness to take himself into the chapel, sit down and just be there. He was capable of nothing more. This conversation has always stayed with me and often my own prayer life has amounted to not much more than a willingness to put myself in a place where I can at least attempt to give God my attention. What seems to count is simply being there and even achieving that little offering has often been a mighty battle for me. I am helped by the illustration which John V. Taylor gives in his book, *The Christlike God*,

> We have lost the gift of a total personal presence which I sometimes encountered in village Africa, where an adult or even a child might enter the room and squat on the floor with no more than an occasional exchange of words or greeting, while I got on with whatever I was doing, until after half an hour or so of simply being together, the visitor would get up saying 'I have seen you' and go.[11]

This simple being present and being attentive to God is at the heart of prayer. I like to think of prayer in this way. Not a whole pile of words and actions, formulas or nagging requests but just a willingness to come into God's presence, to sit with him, to be there. Prayer is about learning to still ourselves so that we can offer our full attention to God, so that we can touch, see, listen, feel and rejoice in the present moment, the only moment in which God can be found.

John V. Taylor describes well how hard we find this:

> We find it so difficult to be inwardly gathered, intent and still, because we are for ever whisking through the present moment, we almost never live in it. We are like champion sprinters in the 100 metres race, leaning forward, pushing our centre of

> gravity several yards ahead, so that if we suddenly become still we should fall flat on our faces. So the world around us, the reality of the present moment, is blurred, unclear, empty in fact, because we have already left it behind. And such a natural thing as simply being here now has become incredibly unnatural to us.[12]

I have challenged a whole list of spiritual directors with my inability to be focused in the present moment. For my part, I only began to learn the lesson through the harsh discipline of illness. For a long period of time I found myself unable to be sure if I would be well enough to, for example, preach a sermon, celebrate communion, take a funeral, chat with a friend, or cook the meal to which I had invited people. The uncertainty was frightening and it was threatening to stop me doing anything at all. Living in the present was the answer to my dilemma. I learnt painfully and slowly that if I was well now, then that was all that mattered. I could live now and not be crippled by the uncertainty of the future. All I had, as indeed all any of us have, if we could only grasp it, was the present moment and if that was good and if it enabled me to do what I longed to do, then I was profoundly grateful and acutely aware of the gift of it. It is a humbling lesson to understand that we are not in control. A similar experience was shared with me by a friend who struggles with ME. She told me that earlier on in her illness she used to think, 'When I am better I will do so and so or be so and so.' Now she says, 'I live for now.'

Aren't we all guilty of this? When I have a baby, when the children are grown-up, when I get promoted or retire, when we have had the kitchen replaced and have bought the new car. So much time and energy is wasted in this way. Learning to give attention to each moment as it comes is what we are challenged to do: the phone call to a colleague, the shopping, the conversation with your daughter, the game of football, the drive to work, the person who is suffering, the meal you are eating, the novel you are reading. We are challenged to be people who can still our lives long enough to give attention. I am now much better physically and, external constraints removed, am trying hard to hang onto what I have learnt. Kat Duff in her book *The Alchemy of Illness* describes, much better than I could, how illness altered her perception:

> I was sitting on the living room couch after a long, tiring morning of work, holding a small bowl of rice in my hands. The phone rang, and – quite out of character – I just sat there and let it ring, as I turned the bowl in my hands and admired its perfect shape. I felt privy to one of the world's great secrets that what *is* is enough, that each moment contains, like the circle of that bowl, the whole of creation in the space it offers, and we need not go anywhere or do anything to find it.[13]

One of the problems for many of us is how to decide in the present moment what is our priority. I for one can make some pretty stupid decisions. Donald Nicholl in his book *Holiness* quotes a story which makes me both smile and wince:

> It concerns a Jewish trader who so grossly overloaded his wagon on which he was to transport his merchandise that his horses could not pull it. He thought of lightening the load by taking off some of the merchandise, but later decided against doing so ... because he felt that each item was indispensable to his career. Still, something had to be done; so he took the wheels off his wagon![14]

Jesus lived his life with a veritable mountain of demands. How did he cope? How did he get his priorities straight, live in the present moment and give the full attention to people and issues which others found so unusual and so disturbing? Many commentators suggest that the second half of chapter 1[15] in Mark's gospel is supposed to convey a specimen day in Jesus' ministry. This makes any day we might have seem like child's play! First Jesus teaches in the synagogue, and then he encounters a man screaming at him, possessed by an evil spirit which he casts out. He is then rushed to the home of Simon Peter's sick mother-in-law whom he heals. Having taught, exorcised and healed most of us would hope for a glass of red wine and to put our feet up, but the consequences for Jesus were quite other. As the news of the healing spread we are told that 'all the people of the town' flocked to his door and he responded to them with compassion, healing many and casting out evil spirits.

Very early the next morning, Jesus got up and went out of the town to a lonely place to pray, to give God his attention. Later the disciples surfaced, found him missing and rushed out to look for him. No doubt they were confused and probably a bit annoyed. They had given up everything to follow this man and now he's really hit the big time but he's just gone off leaving everyone in the lurch. Perhaps he doesn't realise what's happening, they think, so they go in search to tell him the good news of his success. 'Everyone is looking for you, your career's really taken off; they are down there clamouring for your return!' And Jesus refuses. 'We must go to the other villages round here. I have to preach in them also because that is why I came.' His disciples just don't get it. To quit now seems the craziest thing to contemplate. What Jesus did was to say 'no' when we and the disciples would very reasonably have expected him to say, 'Yes! Great I'll be with you just as quickly as I can.'

Jesus was able to say 'no' to one thing so that he was able to say 'yes' to another. He was being realistic about the limitations of being human. Obviously it was deeply important that he should heal suffering people and I am sure that it would have cost him much pain to walk away from such need. However, he knew that he had to set his face to Jerusalem and that even he could not do both. In his solitary place, having taken himself apart to give attention to God in prayer, he was able to sort out his priorities, to use each and every one of his 'present moments' to be obedient to the God who loved him.

What Jesus had to come to terms with, was that his

life, the life of the one who was filled with the fullness of God[16] was also a limited, finite human life, lived out in the small towns of Israel and ultimately to be cruelly cut short. He seemed able to know, understand and indeed embrace these limitations. With his Father's help, he was able to discern the way forward, resisting the need to meet the immediate demands of those in Capernaum or indeed his own need and desire to help and be loved for his success. Jesus, whilst often tempted otherwise, decided to live his life within the human limits which he had embraced.

We are faced with a similar challenge. We too can choose to live in ceaseless struggle to respond to all the infinite demands which surround us, as was the issue for the senior churchman cited above. Undoubtedly, he was doing good things, important things, and worthwhile things, but was he, in all his rush, activity and endeavour, doing the right things … those things which were God's priority for him? We all have to come to terms, sooner or later, with our limitations and make peace with the person we are. *This* particular person, with all its limitations and characteristics. Archbishop Rowan Williams, in a recent lecture, spoke of growing to be 'at home with yourself'.[17] A person really 'at home', who will live realistically with their finitude, gratefully in the present moment, and who will give loving attention to what is before their eyes, themselves, others and God, knowing that each moment is utterly irreplaceable.

Life is not hurrying
on to a
receding future.

nor hankering
after an
imagined past.

It is turning aside,
like Moses,
to the miracle of
the lit bush

to a brightness
that seemed as
transitory as
youth once

but it is the eternity
that awaits you.[18]

Reflection 5

Friendship

The sight of six young, newly ordained deacons carrying, with great dignity, the coffin of their friend down the aisle of Newcastle Cathedral will never leave me. Nor the memory of the wind- and rain-swept cemetery as the same friends, many in tears, carried Simon to his final resting place. Afterwards, we talked together about Simon's life, so devastatingly cut down by epilepsy at the age of twenty-six. I will never forget the following comment: 'It was a privilege to carry him in death as he so often carried us in life.' Simon understood friendship. He valued it, making himself vulnerable to others and being an excellent listener. Simon was someone who connected, who cared. He was a great encourager but could also be an uncomfortable and uncompromising challenger. He saw what was going on for people and he bothered to ask the question or give the affirming comment. He wasn't perfect, far from it, as none of us are, and he carried some heavy burdens, but he was open and willing to be part of this community, to both serve it and to receive from it. In short, he made a difference, a big difference to people's lives. He believed in the importance of relationship.

Relationship, of course, is at the centre of the Christian message although you could be forgiven for not always being aware of that. It can sometimes seem as if the main focus of Christian faith is the Bible and how we interpret it, or worshipping in a particular way, or having spiritual experiences; it is actually about 'a set of relationships: the experience of God's presence among one another and through one another. To embrace the gospel means to enter into a community, the one cannot be obtained without the other.'[1] Christianity is not a magic formula – it is a relationship. It is not about our ability to grasp the concepts – it is about intimacy. It is not about our ability to live good lives – it is about learning to live lives in connection with the God who loves us and with his creation.

Being created in the image of God means, amongst other things, that we find our identity in relationship both with others and with God. This is because part of the nature of God is that he exists in community: Father, Son and Holy Spirit. The divine life itself is relational. From our very beginning as small babies we exist in response to and interaction with others. Being truly human and living in relationship with others are inseparable. Allan Boesak quotes an African proverb which exactly makes this point: 'I am human only because you are human.'[2] The question 'Who am I?' leads straight back to all the people who are part of me, who have formed me for good or ill, all those who have shaped me.

Some we have chosen or have chosen us, others are simply a given of our lives. No one develops in isolation. 'We are woven with varied threads and so often the colours are brought to us and are not of our making.'[3] We are not simply self made but the extent to which we allow people to shape and inform our lives is dependent on the extent to which we are willing and able to engage with others. We are all such provisional creatures who are being formed, and hopefully transformed, as we travel through life. I am reminded of the affirmation of Augustine that 'We have begun to become some great thing.'[4] In his book *The Shape of Living* David Ford uses a marvellous expression: the 'hospitality of the heart'.[5] By this I think he means the extent to which we are willing to open our hearts to receive the other and to allow the boundaries of our own hearts and lives to shift as we respond.

This challenge, the capacity to grow through encounter with others, is as old as life itself, and there is a wonderful exploration of it in the Old Testament in the Book of Job. We find Job, having suffered the devastating loss of all his possessions, his servants, his children and his health, sitting on the ground surrounded by his three friends. They have been silent for seven days and seven nights and as they begin to speak we start to see that their silence was much preferable. The basic problem is that Job's friends all see the world through the same filter. It is as follows: 'everything comes from God, and God is just; because he is just, he rewards the good and punishes the bad; therefore those who prosper must be good, and those who suffer must be bad.'[6] This is obviously pretty bad news for someone with Job's problems!

Job, however, whilst he has always up until now also seen things through the same filter, knows that in his case things are not following the rules. He starts to tell them his truth but the friends block him, running for cover. They cannot risk hearing what he is saying because if they do they will have to change their equation, their view of the world, which they are hanging on to with all their strength. One by one they take Job on and there is not a speck of 'hospitality of the heart' in sight. They sacrifice the truth of Job's circumstances and any compassion which they might offer to him so that they can maintain their ordered view of faith, so that they do not in any way need to amend the borders of their being. But Job is not having it. His response is, in effect, 'You don't understand. You're not feeling my feelings. All your words are not of the slightest use to me.' Because his friends will not take the risk of entering into the reality of Job's experience, of thinking for a second that what Job is saying is the truth, they can go on trusting in their simplistic teaching.

All Job wants is that one, just one of them, might take the risk of offering sympathetic understanding, of seeing things as they appear to him and of walking the way with him through this desolate time of his life. Job is crying out (as we all do inwardly if not always outwardly) for someone to understand him and his dilemma, but none of them will do it. None of them will take the scary step into the complex reality of Job's new situation – a situation which scares Job as well! For me this scenario is echoed in my counselling practice. Each client I have worked with, though some more than others, invites me to walk with them, to see the world as it is from their perspective. Sometimes, especially if issues of faith are concerned, you take the step of entering their world with trepidation, not knowing if you will come out of the process with your faith intact. You cannot work with people in any other way. If they are to change, the encounter must be real. If it is real it will change you too.

To Job's so-called friends, it seems inconceivable that an honest hearing of Job's position might, just might, make them reconsider *their* grasp on the world, *their* theology and *their* friendship and that they might have to amend their theological understanding in the light of new evidence and forge a new friendship with a more open acceptance and a deeper vulnerability. I am reminded of a Peanuts cartoon quoted in Bob Fyall's helpful book on Job in which Lucy says to Charlie Brown, 'there is one thing you're going to have to learn: you reap what you sow, you get out of life what you put in.' Snoopy mutters in reply: 'I'd kinda like to see a little more margin for error.'[7] Job's friends admit no margin of error, nor will they allow any deviation from their norms. There is humility lacking here and fear is beginning to show.

The 'friends' have every reason to be fearful and to vigorously fight their corner. Job's refusal to concede any of their arguments and explanations makes them very angry and vulnerable. What if he is right? What then? Then their comfortable and predictable worldview would also be threatened. They would have to rethink, and change the boundaries of their being and this is not what they want to do. There is precious little 'hospitality of the heart' being offered to Job. Before we leave Job with his tormentors it is salutary to recall that at the end of this story God is furious with the 'friends' for failing to speak the truth about him. It is a book which sets itself against those who withhold the hospitality of their hearts; against those who hurt the weak and the poor by their judgements and who hold to their religious opinions at the expense of offering love and compassion to those who are suffering. Trevor Dennis helpfully reminds us that, 'Jesus will pick up the cudgels of this great writer in his confrontations with the scribes and the Pharisees in the Gospels.'[8]

Deep encounters always transform us and those of us who try to follow the Christian way will know that we are called to live out that transformation in community. We would often like another way, an easier way to become holy, a more controllable way to live out the Christian life. No wonder we try to escape into other things. We deflect our energies into rigorous study of the Bible, elaborate and well-executed performance of liturgy, intellectual argument about how we should live, silence and withdrawal but all roads lead back inexorably to the same context: that of community, that of relationship.

In the theological college where I work, we study together, pray together, eat together, and worship together, argue together and share the task of ordinary daily living together. This gives ample opportunity to discover just how messy and testing community life can be. Each year a new enthusiastic crop of ordinands turns up, excited at the prospect of living in this Christian community, but it doesn't take long to discover that perfection is a long way off. We find that our Christian brothers and sisters, even (or perhaps especially) those heading for ordination, are uncomfortable companions. It soon seems to us that we would do better somewhere else. This particular group of people are very wacky, this place is particularly unreal and odd. 'I will be fine', students say, 'when I am in the parish.' Unfortunately, holiness does not begin next week, or in a different context or with other people, it begins today, here in this place with these people. As Margaret Silf so powerfully puts it in her book *Landmarks*: 'Wherever you are, however unchosen, is the place of blessing.'[9] We must stop looking for the ideal community and start living in the one in which we find ourselves – a community inevitably full of unsatisfactory people just like ourselves.

We cannot grow as people until we learn to appreciate the other and that is why 'hospitality of the heart' through friendship is so important to us in our journey. The delight of friendship is in learning to appreciate and to enjoy the other and learning to be appreciated and enjoyed by another. It is about both sharing our commonality and our difference. As we come to understand a friend better we start to look at the world through fresh eyes. We are drawn out of ourselves beyond the confines of our own narrow world into the sometimes vastly different world of the other. This is well illustrated in a quotation from *To Kill a Mockingbird*, 'You never really understand a person until you consider things from his point of view … until you climb into his skin and walk around in it.'[10]

Most of my closest friends are really quite like me. I suppose we naturally choose those we understand and find easily compatible but such friendships do not deeply challenge our hospitality of the heart. Friendship on the other hand with someone very different, whether in personality, race or religion can be very challenging indeed. It can take a huge effort of communication to listen and to try to understand the world as the other finds it. However, such a friendship is worth the effort because it will really extend our experience and understanding. I have a close friend who is not much like me and who has a rather different approach to life. The other day we were discussing a party we had both attended. She is very happy to be an observer. She enjoys weighing things up from the outside and is cautious of being involved. I, on the other hand, usually find myself at the heart of things, getting stuck in. I guess most of us could align ourselves in some way with these two positions or see where we are between them. It has been most enlightening to learn to see things from her point of view. Life certainly seems different if you are standing on the edge looking in and I have learnt a lot. She would also say that she has gained in understanding, for observing only gets you so far and hearing first hand what is going on has changed her perception. Either way, whichever position you naturally take up in life, you only have limited vision on your own. It was as if we had both been at different parties!

To engage in friendship then extends our world. It opens us to the unexpected and whilst it can be invigorating such hospitality also involves great risk, as Job's friends understood. As we engage with the other we are taken into their experience of life. We see things as they are for them, their assumptions, their dreams, their fears, their limitations, their judgements, their aspirations and as we do this we are forced to question our own way of seeing, to examine what we have always taken for granted. The view from the edge when we are used to being in the middle of things is confusing and disorientating at first but as we settle down it can help us to see and understand things anew. The possibilities of this are beautifully expressed in a book called *Hospitality to the Stranger* by Thomas Ogletree:

> Strangers have stories to tell which we have never heard before, stories which can redirect our seeing and stimulate our imaginations. Their stories invite us to view the world from a novel perspective. They display the finitude and relativity of our own orientation to meaning ... The stranger does not simply challenge or subvert our assumed world of meaning; she may enrich, even transform, that world.[11]

Of course in friendship, this is a two-way process, a shaping, challenging and enlarging of each others' worlds.

Many people live almost their whole lives with very low expectations of friendship. For whatever reason they are not prepared to take a chance with another to risk the kind of vulnerability by which, in Ogletree's terms, a stranger is turned into a friend. If we do not take the risk of friendship we are making our world smaller, limiting our experience of the other and thus our possibilities of growth. Our journey towards wholeness ultimately comes not only from ourselves but from those others we allow to become part of our lives. We gain in maturity not by 'overcoming the other but by being in relationship with them,'[12] from seeing them first and foremost as gift. Of course the truth is that none of us can be just gift, we can also be irritation or at worst threat. Usually, we are a mixture, of both trust and vulnerability, hope and anxiety, exasperation and delight in the lives of those with whom we engage. Sadly, as sinful creatures we don't have a perfect other to offer! So the challenge of friendship is to work to allow all that is gift to triumph over all that which might destroy, to help people to flourish and not to damage them. It is a very fragile balance at times and the balance is shifted by betrayal of trust, by hurts going unacknowledged and unforgiven, by the gift being taken for granted. To return to the African proverb quoted earlier, 'I am human only because you are human' implies that if we turn away from others we, in a sense, start to disappear. The Christian view is that we cannot be unless we are in relationship. Simone Weil speaks of this in her book *Waiting for God*. 'She suggests that all of us are people in waiting; we wait for the attention or recognition of others not just to acknowledge our self or to confirm ourselves as good, but to gift us with a sense of self only another's love can provide. We wait to be befriended.'[13] Indeed we need to be befriended to grow. Friendships are not simply something which we have, rather, they are one of the main shapers of who we are and of who we will become.

It has taken me a long time to understand that the Christian life is anything much to do with friendship. It simply isn't a topic that the Church seems to place much emphasis upon. We talk endlessly about the importance of the family, we briefly nod to the importance of friendship when engaged in our ferocious and dishonouring debates on human sexuality, but no one has ever implied to me that friendship is an important way in which I could grow as a Christian.

I suppose that I had always associated Jesus with such exalted terms as prophet, priest, Lord and King. Somehow this had put Jesus at a distance and obscured for me the possibility of Jesus as friend. Of course, there were the obvious hymns such as 'What a friend we have in Jesus' but somehow these were acquainted with my childhood years and it seemed a cosy concept which I should shed as I grew up. The importance and centrality of friendship had not been disclosed. This is particularly strange if you read the gospels with your eyes open for signs of friendship. What do you find but Jesus with a group of friends wandering around and sharing communal life? A group of friends whom he loves, who chat together, argue together, eat together, ponder together and who vie with each other for attention and status as they try to make sense of what is happening to them. A group of friends who matter to each other and who rely on each other for support and care. Jesus gives his life for his friends, and because of this the disciples cease to be servants and become friends with Jesus and through that friendship become friends with God. 'No longer do I call you servants, for a servant does not know what his master is about. I have called you friends, because I have disclosed to you everything that I heard from my Father.'[14] This is an extraordinary turn of events. No longer do we experience the obedient relationship of servant to master or the dependent relationship of child to parent. Instead, we are called into friendship with God and will grow in that friendship as we follow his command to become the friend of others.

The Church then is simply those who are the friends of Jesus. Of course, friendship in our society is usually about being with those who think like us, live like us and quite simply are like us. This is a comfortable splitting into 'alike' groups and is not at all what this gospel imperative is about. This closed idea of friendship is outrageously challenged by Jesus as he makes a priority of being a friend of prostitutes and sinners. This contemptuous description unintentionally reveals the truth about Jesus; it reveals Jesus' friendship to the unlikeable, the unacceptable, and the unrighteous. It reveals Jesus' willingness to engage in friendship even with the likes of you and me. It is difficult to think of a less equal or appropriate friendship for the Son of God than that; the unlimited hospitality of God's heart offered to me and his acceptance of the finite hospitality of mine. Through this act he challenges us not to be exclusive in our friendships; not just to offer friendship to people like ourselves. He is asking us to offer an open acceptance and affection towards all people and a willingness to learn from them. This mutuality is key to friendship and was found in the friendship of Jesus with his disciples, who mattered to him and whom he needed. This was most evident in Gethsemane where the disciples' failure to support him through this agony hurt him painfully.[15] Such mutuality is disconcerting especially when it is with the Son of God. If friendship with God is mutual then it is uncomfortable to ponder how our relationship with him touches God's heart, but that is exactly the form of relationship which Jesus describes. It is a vulnerable, risk-taking project of love, a costly uncertain offer of close relationship which we are perfectly at liberty to reject and which we often do.

In addition to mutuality, friendship flourishes within faithfulness and commitment. We cannot make the promise to a friend that we will always feel friendship and love for them because we cannot command our feelings in that way. There will inevitably be times when we let our friends down, when we irritate and perplex them, times when we simply don't agree or when we get less pleasure in each other's company, which is inevitable sometimes in friendships which endure over a long period of time. Clearly, we cannot promise to command our feelings but what we can promise is to keep faith with our friends, to walk the way with them and to act in friendship to them, come what may.

Judas was Jesus' friend, one of those very close to him, who had shared a corporate life over several years. Even as Judas was in the very act of handing over Jesus with a kiss, Jesus still claimed him as his friend. He did not cast him off. 'Friend,' he said 'do what you have to do.'[16] I cannot believe that Jesus' commitment to Judas faltered even at this, any more than his commitment to us falters in the serial betrayals in our own lives. Ruth Etchells sums this up for me, in her moving poem, 'The Ballad of the Judas Tree':

(*He descended into Hell ... and preached to the spirits there.*)

In Hell there grew a Judas tree
Where Judas hanged and died
Because he could not bear to see
His Master crucified.

The Lord descended into Hell
And found His Judas there,
Forever hanging on the tree
Grown from his own despair.

So Jesus cut His Judas down
Took him in His arms,
It was for this I came, He said
And not to do you harm.

My Father gave me twelve good men
And all of them I've kept,

Though one betrayed and one denied
Some fled and others slept.

In three days' time I shall return
To make the others glad
But first I had to come to Hell
To share the death you had.

My tree will grow in place of yours
Its roots strike here as well
There is no final victory
Without this soul from Hell.

So when we all condemn him
As of every traitor worst
Remember that of all His men
Our Lord forgave him first.[17]

In his relationship with Judas, Jesus experiences the reality of friendship, not as an idealised, perfect friendship but one which is painful and messy. For Judas we see how passionate commitment can slip into equally passionate destruction. Jesus' death reminds us that relationships can fail, that misunderstanding can flourish, that our hopes can be crushed, that sin both individual and corporate can conspire to prevent and damage friendship. The Resurrection then, stands as a promise from the Trinity, itself a 'community of persons in relationship',[18] a living out of friendship, that the forces which drive us apart, which make us strangers rather than friends, which conspire against friendship, will not ultimately triumph. It is exactly as we align ourselves with the power of this promise, as we commit ourselves in friendships, open and vulnerable, that we can become sacraments of God's love in his world.

Reflection 6

Success and Failure

The telephone caller was really despondent. She was a high-flying accountant in a very well-thought-of firm and was used to going steadily up the ladder but lately things hadn't been going so well. She'd failed to get several promotions and now she was being offered a golden handshake, one which most of us would have jumped at. Her instant reaction, however, had been to try for equivalent jobs and now she was ringing me because these hadn't been forthcoming either. The gloom and sense of failure were palpable. Where was God in all this? For this woman success had built on success and she was very well-thought-of at work, at home and at church. How then was it possible for this state of affairs to be doing so much damage to her sense of self? How could it be undermining her confidence so much? All she could see was failure. She had no ability initially to see the gift, the gift of the opportunities which this opened up. Why was this?

It is absolutely proper to have a great sense of achievement over a job well done and to feel a deep sense of satisfaction at the success of a venture, and it is pure gold if we can offer the achievement to God and praise God for the gift of it. However, success must be held very lightly indeed! The danger is that we can become so needy of success that this simple transaction of gift from God and the thanks due becomes corrupted. If we become used to doing well and it becomes what we expect, almost as a right, then success can become a problem. We may no longer focus on the challenge of what we can do with the gifts we have, but let success start to define who we are and, much worse, whether we are OK or not. Success begins to mesmerise us, becoming a recognition we deeply need from others and one without which we cannot happily live, instead of a personal joy at a job well done. We become success junkies driven by an almost insatiable hunger to do well but then needing to keep this up if we are to feel OK. This can start to undermine us. When success is necessary for our wellbeing then it becomes a tyrant who drives us hard and never, apart from for fleeting moments, gets us to a better place. It becomes a kind of addiction which is always demanding but only leaves us satisfied for a brief moment before reasserting its needs again.

Our society runs on the delusion of the importance of success. How hard we strive to look good and to succeed. We divide the world into those who succeed and those who fail and this greatly influences how we see ourselves. We assess and compare ourselves according to a whole range of attributes: appearance, age, gender, qualifications, wealth, and personality. Life trains us to make assessments – professional, sexual, social, on a hierarchical scale of reference which lets us see where we are relative to the other. She has a bigger house, but I have a newer car. She has designer clothes, but I have a better figure. She has a better figure, but the men like me more. He gets paid more, but I am more intelligent. He is more intelligent, but I've got a stronger personality. He's got a stronger personality, but I'm more loveable. We find ourselves on different ladders in different situations; for example, you may find yourself located differently in terms of success in your family compared to your job. You may feel more successful in one context than another and all this is, of course, incredibly precarious because you are at the mercy of external events. You may, as the woman described above, feel well placed in the success stakes, but then find that an arbitrary event like redundancy or illness, or the failure to get promoted, or your partner's affair, or your child's bullying dislodges you from the position you held and makes you feel more a failure than a success.

What is common to these experiences is that they are all relative, i.e. you are more successful or less successful than others. The woman described above was, in the eyes of most people who knew her, very successful but chose to judge herself against those who had got the jobs which she had not. In addition, success is always temporary. Some people may be successful over a very long period but since success is always referenced from outside and is always relative, finally they will have to give way even if that is just because of retirement or ageing. Success in the world's terms is at best a neutral thing and can be at worst a very negative thing. Henri Nouwen writes in his book *In the Name of Jesus* that his success as a writer was 'putting his soul in danger'.[1] The accountant had found that failure exposed her success for what it was: a huge distraction from getting on with the real business of life which is learning to live in the grace of God. Her success had shored her up, it had kept people off and had colluded with her in avoiding asking the really deep questions which were now starkly posed. This is a potentially frightening place to be and her first instinct was exactly as mine would have been – to escape back into the known. But as this was blocked too she had to sit with all of this and it was very painful indeed. Suddenly there was time and necessity to confront herself and to see what was there, 'What good would it do you to get everything you want and lose you, the real you? What could you ever trade your soul for?'[2] Our moments of failure are real opportunities for growth and gradually she saw that there were gifts in this situation, there was the freedom to think out of the box, to dream different dreams and to live a new life. She made some very brave decisions about the future and has moved into different work, work which has made good use of all her experience but which has been personally very life-giving.

Being fully human, it was inevitable that Jesus would be confronted with similar issues. As soon as he was baptised he was driven into the wilderness where he had three demons to face.[3] Amongst other things they raised questions about success, about power and influence and about the rightful priority of God in his life. We too need to confront these demons and if we haven't we can be sure that they will be very influential in our lives. We must also remember that Jesus' harshest words were to the Pharisees who were sure they were right and to those who were more concerned about possessions than people. Both these groups have much to protect and the gospels make it clear that the only people who can easily accept God are those with nothing to protect and these are called the 'poor' in the gospels. The poor and unsuccessful are close to God's heart so we need to go to them to learn more of God. The rich and successful on the other hand find it harder to respond.

Jesus was just setting out on a journey when a rich young man ran up to him and asked him: 'Good Teacher, what must I do to win eternal life?'[4] He is concerned here primarily with *himself*, with *his* future, with *his* perfectibility. Jesus in reply lists the commandments but surprisingly slips in one which is not usually there: 'Do not defraud.' Where did that come from? We can only imagine it was a gentle dig at the questioner who then leaps in to prove that despite his wealth he is speaking with serious religious intent. 'Teacher, all these I have kept since I was a boy.' In other words he is quite a success! Jesus looks at him and loves him. He knows that at heart this is a good lad, but one who is trapped by the circumstances of his successful life. He needs to be freed and Jesus tells him how, 'Go, sell everything you have, and give to the poor.'[5] This is clearly not what he wanted or expected to hear. It is too much. It is too hard and he walks away.

Compare this to another encounter with Jesus which is recorded later in the same chapter of Mark, that of Blind Bartimaeus.[6] Unlike the respectful approach of the rich young man, Bartimaeus shouts at Jesus. He has no time for polite small talk, no proprieties to defend and he really riles those around him by his pushiness. He has nothing to protect and nothing to lose. He knows he's empty and he is in great need. Jesus stops and calls him, surprising everyone by his apparent interest in such an unimportant person. Bartimaeus doesn't need to be asked twice, he's up on his feet throwing his cloak aside and rushing to Jesus' side. 'What do you want me to do for you?' Jesus asks because he can see that he can give this man something. There's an openness, a desperate neediness unlike the young man who is covering himself and weighing up what he will do. 'Rabbi, I want to see.' There is no alternative for him, he will not walk away because he cannot. He is not weighed down by the burdens of success.

So, paradoxically, we have in this one chapter of Mark a rich young man who thinks that he can see God's way but who is actually blind, and a blind man who can actually see. The rich young man cannot see that he no longer needs to pursue success in his disciplined religious life, and that the accumulating of spiritual success by more and more effort is not what God wants of him. He is challenged to give up all the trappings of success and then to follow Jesus, but he walks away. By contrast, Bartimaeus, who for all we know may never have done a good thing in his life, could see that to follow Jesus was the one essential thing and he did not walk away but followed him.[7]

Learning to see clearly is such a necessity of the Christian life as we struggle to live counter-culturally. Mostly, we work with the world's way of seeing success and failure and what we have to learn is to see in God's way. When we first moved to Durham I was training for the ministry for three years and with two small children we were not very well off. We actually lived in a lovely house which came with my husband's job but it was chaotic inside: the carpet didn't match the suite, and the suite didn't match the curtains and the curtains didn't … and so on, it was a jangle of mismatching colours and patterns. I am sad to say that I was embarrassed about this. I felt exposed as I visited the beautifully appointed houses of my friends and when they visited me I was quick to explain that the house was not ours, and so forth. I did not want them to think that I thought it was OK as it was. Perish the thought! Then one day one of my children's young friends came in after school with her mum for a cup of tea and a chat. She was a single young mum, struggling to make ends meet and not from the posher part of Durham in which I was lucky enough to live. She walked into my living room and was stopped in her tracks by what she saw. 'What a brilliant view you've got. It's beautiful and this room is huge. What a wonderful house.' In a fleeting moment she had done what the 'poor' always do, she had seen the truth of things and had made me see it too. I never apologised again for the way things looked in that house. What was failure for me was success for her and I only needed to be taught a different way of seeing to get it. Embarrassment was turned into a humble thankfulness for what I had been given.

This different way of seeing was something that was always making the disciples flounder. Why, after all, would Jesus choose to spend time with a poor, inconsequential blind beggar rather than an important and influential rich young man? Jesus was always striving to make them see, to teach them to see as God sees. To show them that it could be done differently. Most importantly he was trying to prepare them for the 'failure' which was to come. In the gospels he keeps telling them in different ways that he must die, that he will 'fail', that he must allow this to happen and the disciples just don't get it! Jesus must often have despaired of them as they fought for the privileged position, showed off, panicked and despaired and ultimately in their different ways abandoned or betrayed him. So much failure to see the way but Jesus was to show them what God can do with failure.

While writing this I was interested to find that in a nationwide poll to discover Britain's favourite poem, the clear and unassailable winner was Rudyard Kipling's 'If'. This is a poem all about success and failure but I was particularly struck by,

> If you can meet with Triumph and Disaster,
> And treat these two impostors just the same.[8]

Impostors are not what they seem, so again we are being challenged to look at things differently. Success and failure are seen as equal in some way which is not immediately obvious. Success as explored earlier dazzles us so we can't see reality, especially the reality of who we are. What then can failure do for us?

Failure can free us from illusion and help us to take a good long look at our reality. It can help us to find out who we really are, something that many of us, and especially successful people, never do. Success helps us to avoid the necessary humiliation of finding ourselves naked. If nothing else, failure can potentially free us from ourselves and from our illusions. I can remember many years ago getting really irritated with the counsellor I was seeing at the time. Mary kept asking me, 'Judy, who are you?' I see clearly now that I kept answering in terms of externals and she would simply put the question again. At the time it really exasperated me but now, 20 years on, at last I can see what she was getting at. She wanted to know who Judy was when all of what I did was removed, who I was essentially. Henri Nouwen writes of a similar experience whilst living in a l'Arche Community:

> The first thing that struck me when I came to live in a house with mentally handicapped people was that their liking or disliking of me had absolutely nothing to do with any of the many useful things I had done until then. Since nobody could read my books, they could not impress anyone, and since most of them never went to school, my 20 years at

> Notre Dame, Yale and Harvard did not provide a significant introduction. My considerable ecumenical experience proved even less valuable. When I offered some meat to one of the assistants during dinner, one of the handicapped men said to me, 'Don't give him meat, he doesn't eat meat, he's a Presbyterian.' Not being able to use any of the skills that had proved so practical in the past was a real source of anxiety. I was suddenly faced with my naked self, open for affirmations and rejections, hugs and punches, smiles and tears, all dependent simply on how I was perceived at the moment. In a way, it seemed as though I was starting life all over again. Relationships, connections, reputations could no longer be counted on.[9]

None of us likes to confront ourselves because it makes us very fearful of what we will find. Failure encourages us to look, although even then it is not inevitable that we will choose to do so. Failure can be such a good teacher and so I suspect that God is nowhere near as concerned with failure as we are; indeed, his provision of forgiveness always potentially makes failure into a gracious and enabling new way forward.

To grow in holiness we need to escape from any notion that we can make ourselves perfect. If we fail and are confronted with our limitations, we can begin to see who we are and what we need and this makes it easier to come to God just as it was easier for Bartimaeus than for the successful young man. The place of failure is potentially the place of learning and it is there that we will discover some unexpected things about ourselves. Failure is God's chance to open us and to stretch us beyond our tiny hopes and expectations but often we simply get so bogged down in them that we can't see a way forward.

I have always been interested in the 'Road to Emmaus' story in Luke's gospel[10] because it exactly catches these two followers of Jesus in the throes of coming to terms with failure. They had obviously been with Jesus who had excited and inspired them, and who had raised all sorts of hopes for their lives. He had won their love and commitment and then total, abject failure and disaster had struck. Here we find them trudging along the road, going home with their dreams shattered and probably returning to lots of people who will be just longing to say, 'I told you so.' (There is never any shortage of people willing to glory in the failure of those with the guts to pursue their dreams!) What were they to make of these terrible events? How could they pick themselves up and go on? Jesus, as he does with us all if only we had the eyes to see, is walking with them in the failure, gently trying to make them understand. He goes over the Scriptures trying to get them to set their feelings in a broader context, to begin to see things with the eyes and priorities of God. Let all this go, he says, because God's love for you is greater than you can imagine. Through the glory of Easter he can transform everything. In this way we too are encouraged to let go of all the myriad little deaths of our lives into the hands of the God of Easter. We need to understand that

Christ could transform failure only by failing himself.

So we too must learn to live with the double character of the Christian life: abundant life and yet many little deaths, failure which can bear more fruit than success. Always we must hold the two in tension as is beautifully and simply expressed in this poem of Ralph Wright:

Two trees
proclaim in spring
a word to the world

one exploding
into blossom
trumpets glory

one stretching
dead limbs
holds the empty
body of God

both speak
with due reserve
into the listening
ear of the world.[11]

This double character is also the truth of our lives. Success and failure do not alternate tidily in our lives but are both in us in a complex way. We are shown this in the 'wheat and tares' parable in Matthew's gospel.[12] The farmhands ask if they should get rid of the weeds and the farmer replies, 'No, for in gathering the weeds you would uproot the wheat along with them. Let both of them grow together until the harvest; and at harvest time I will tell the reapers, collect the weeds first and bind them in bundles to be burned, but gather the wheat into my barn.' Somehow success and failure are necessarily linked. We can enjoy success which we know is tainted with failure: the promotion which is built at least partly on the backs of the people we have criticised and undermined, and the excellent exam result which was bought at the expense of all the legitimate needs of others which we ignored. Equally, we can experience failure when we know that at least some of the motivation was good: the feeling of failure as a parent when your child goes off the rails even though you know that you have rescued and forgiven them many times before; the promotion which was not received because you spoke unwelcome truths about the running of the organisation. Two biblical characters who epitomise this interpenetration of success and failure exactly are David in the Old Testament and Peter in the New Testament.

David was a phenomenal success but was also vulnerable to the most terrible failures. He was a multi-talented man, a passionate man, a risk taker who lived and loved life to the full and trusted God. I guess he also failed, as people taking the risk of living life to the full often do, but the accounts we have of David in the Old Testament, tend, as any eulogy does, to gloss over the failures. However, even these accounts are harshly honest about his failure with Bathsheba, the adultery followed by his attempts to cover his responsibility for her pregnancy, and the disgraceful murder of her husband, the loyal and brave Uriah.[13] David, as so often happens to us, having failed once by sleeping with Bathsheba (or even by entertaining the thought of making love to her) then got trapped into a whole train of events which gathered their own momentum and justification, so much so that he completely lost the plot and was unable to see himself as he was. This happened to such an extent that even when Nathan rebukes David with this story he still cannot connect it with himself:

> In a certain town there lived two men, one rich, the other poor. The rich man had large flocks and herds; the poor man had nothing of his own except one little ewe lamb he had bought. He reared it, and it grew up in his home together with his children. It shared his food, drank from his cup, and nestled in his arms; it was like a daughter to him. One day a traveller came to the rich man's house, and he, too mean to take something from his own flock or herd to serve his guest, took the poor man's lamb and served that up.[14]

The Bible tells us graphically that David's immediate response was that he 'burned with anger against the man'[15] who had done this thing and said that he deserved to die. Still the penny does not drop! Often the real stories of our own lives are just as deeply hidden so that we can no longer hear them. We are all excellent at putting our story out publicly in such a form that we hide our responsibility. Too weary and too preoccupied with our complex lives it is just easier to put a much better gloss on things than we deserve. The problem is when we come to believe it. Often, as good friends or as counsellors, it is our job to suggest an alternative story to challenge the truth of what is being told, not to collude. Nathan must have feared for his life at this juncture. David, after all, had already ruthlessly removed one obstacle; an irksome prophet would seem to be a second temptation. However, Nathan goes ahead and accuses David directly: 'You are the man!' It is at this point that the calibre of David shows. Once the truth gets through to him he is much too honest and knows himself too well to blame anyone else.

Blaming is an instinctive human response to failure and sadly it is the principal response which blocks the possibility of failure being transformative. What is not owned is not transforming. So often failure does not open up a way to growth and understanding. I think of the husband whose wife has left him for another man taking the children with her and breaking up the family home. He is understandably angry with her for abandoning him, and with the 'other man' for his part, and certainly there is responsibility there. However, he will get nowhere until he can own his own part of the blame in the situation, his responsibility for the failure of the marriage, and bring it into God's presence for healing and of course forgiveness. The Lord's Prayer rings in our ears: 'Forgive us our sins, for we too forgive all who have done us wrong.'[16] I think of the woman who always finds herself in unsatisfactory work relationships whatever the context. There are always unreasonable bosses and unreliable assistants, people who criticise and gossip and colleagues who are unsupportive. Of course, some of this must be so, but if the blame is only external and this woman does not own her personal part in the breakdown of relationships then there is no possibility again of learning from the failures. David did not blame others, but owned the situation he had created. Once he had realised his failures, he was not much concerned with his public image but was able to go straight to the heart of the matter. 'I have sinned against the Lord,'[17] says David to Nathan: I have failed in the fullest sense because I have failed the God who loves me. So David, capable of great goodness, but deeply flawed, asks for forgiveness and this is given, but not without bitter consequences. In 2 Samuel[18] we find him doing everything he can to save the life of his baby son, pleading with God in prayer for his son's life, fasting and sleeping on the floor, but the baby dies. David accepts this and gets up, washes and dresses and goes to worship God. This offers us a case study in failure and success in prayer. David pours his desire out to God in prayer, but is able to let God be the ultimate judge of what is right. He accepts the outcome and gets on with his life.

Like David, Peter's failures are fruitful because they bring him powerfully into the heart of God. Peter frequently misunderstands, relies on his own strength, shows poor judgement of himself and is often prone to being completely over the top! However, his qualification to lead the new Christian community is not his successes, such as the time he alone recognises exactly who Jesus is,[19] nor his failures, for we would all equally qualify there, but his response to his failures. His qualification to share the ministry of a 'failed' Messiah is that he has been drawn deeply into the mystery of failure and through it has known God's love and forgiveness. Peter did fail big time, but his failure did not cause him to doubt God, or to reject God, or to blame God. Rather, his failure led him to learn the extent of God's love for him and the extent of his own weakness. He crashed down far enough to be empty and hungry for the love of so selfless and humble a God, down far enough that he could see his truth. When Peter was making all sorts of exalted claims about his commitment to Jesus in the face of adversity,[20] Jesus knew that he would be unable to deliver, that he would fail. However, Jesus then tells Peter that he has prayed for him, 'that your faith may not fail. And when you have turned back, strengthen your brothers.'[21]

This is at the heart of failure. We too will fail but if we can make this failure an opportunity to come to God open-handedly in our need and to meet him there, then our faith and confidence in God's love will grow. Such experiences will help us, as they did Peter, to turn to others in their failure and to give them strength and show compassion. It is always those who have known 'forgiven failure' to whom people turn in need. Their wounded vulnerability makes them attractive companions on life's journey and their consciousness of failure keeps them humble and unwilling to judge others. As Francis of Assisi once said, we need to go to the place of failure, to learn to 'embrace the leper within before we can embrace the leper outside.'[22] We need to learn to show compassion to ourselves before we will be able to show compassion to others.

One possible response to fear of failure is simply to give up trying, to take no risks so that you court no failure. Such a risk-averse life would itself be a failure and many people idolise security so much that this is exactly how they live. Small, protected, limited, closed lives which aren't unkind or harmful but which are not open and generous and so reflect little of the gracious God we are called to serve. I am reminded of a poster of a ship in harbour which one of my friends had as a student many years ago. The caption was 'A ship is safe in harbour but it is not what ships are for.' If we are to grow to become fully human then we need to trust our hearts and experience and to take risks. True wisdom, as Jesus tells us, demands the finding of a narrow and dangerous way and sometimes when we risk and try we will fail, but that is how true maturity is learnt. Here, as in so much else, the tax collectors, drunkards and prostitutes have the advantage over us. We often need hard circumstances to persuade us to risk moving on and their circumstances are hard already. I am always amazed at how hard it is for us to risk change. People come to me whose lives are painfully inadequate but they still cling on, unprepared to risk trying something different. Better the devil you know than the God you don't! That is why sometimes crises can be a real blessing as they give no choice but to risk change and often that can lead to new life.

Truly new things are always beset with risk. Setting out to write your first book; playing a clarinet solo for the first time; new relationships; new jobs; having a baby; your first driving lesson; the first time you let your child walk to school alone; the surgery you undergo and the first time you stand in front of a class to teach. God too started a truly new work in creation and by taking the fearful risk of giving us freedom there will always be precariousness in the venture. By engaging through love he leaves us free to respond or not, as a response of love can never be forced or required. We are made for God who pours himself out in love for us but we can refuse the strongest pull of our being and lock ourselves away in hatred and self-centredness. It is possible. We are free to choose it and some, it seems, do.

If we choose to share the risk of God's creation, we will be being made new ourselves. Every time, in the company of God, that we face something which is hard to face: commit ourselves to some venture; risk thinking out of the box; struggle with a challenge that takes all our strength and courage, and we succeed, then we are playing our part in God's creation. Every time we do our best and fail, every time we have to endure one of the many little deaths which life brings to us, but allow God to take the failure into Christ, then we are part of God's work of creation. Every time we can look at life and see it as it is, a strange mixture of success and failure all gently held in the love of God, we will be given a hint of Christ's resurrection work and we will, by God's grace, be part of it.

God's work of art.
That's me?
Then beauty must lie
In the eye of the
Beholder.

I feel more like
One of those statues
Michelangelo left
Half emerging
From the marble block;
Full of potential
On the verge of life,
But prisoned still
By circumstance and
Fear.

Yet part of me is free –
And you are still creating,
Bringing to life
The promise that is there.
Sometimes by
Hammer blows
Which jar my being,
Sometimes by
Tender strokes half felt
Which waken me to
Life.

Go on Lord.
Love me into wholeness.
Set me free
To share with you
In your creative joy;
To laugh with you
At your delight
In me,
Your work of art.[23]

Notes

Introduction

1. Anthony Bloom (Metropolitan Anthony of Sourozh), *Beginning to Pray*, Paulist Press, 1970, p. 2.
2. Luke 18:9–14.
3. Arsenius 36 as quoted in Rowan Williams, *Silence and Honey Cakes*, Lion Publishing, 2003, p. 44.
4. Lewis Carroll, *Alice's Adventures in Wonderland*, Blackie & Son, (1865), p. 25.
5. Francis Dewar, *Invitations*, SPCK, 1996, p. 15.
6. 2 Corinthians 12:10.
7. Richard Rohr, *Simplicity*, Crossroad Publishing, 1990, p. 117.
8. Athenagoras (Ecumenical Patriarch of Constantinople) as quoted in Jean Vanier, *Finding Peace*, Continuum, 2003, p. 59.

Refection 1: Hiding from God

1. Luke 17:11–19.
2. Luke 17:13.
3. Luke 17:14.
4. Yehuda Amichai, *The Selected Poetry of Yehuda Amichai*, University of California Press, 1996, p. 34.
5. Dag Hammarskjöld, *Markings*, Faber and Faber Ltd, 1964, p. 2.
6. *Methodist Worship Book*, Methodist Publishing House, 1999, p. 290.
7. Stephen Conway, *Living the Eucharist*, DLT, 2001, p. 74.
8. Luke 22:42.
9. ibid.

10. George Appleton, *Daily Prayer and Praise*, The Lutterworth Press, 1962.
11. Mike Yaconelli, *Messy Spirituality*, Hodder and Stoughton, 2001, p. 16.
12. Gerard W. Hughes, *God of Surprises*, DLT, 1985, p. 36.
13. 1 John 4:18, New English Bible, OUP/CUP, 1972.
14. Trevor Dennis, *The Three Faces of God*, Triangle SPCK, 1999, pp. 81–84.

Refection 2: Dealing with our Desires

1. Martin Nystrom, Restoration Music/Sovereign Lifestyle Music, 1983. No 27 in *Songs of Fellowship*, Kingsway Music, 1991.
2. W. B. Yeats, 'Aedh wishes for the Cloths of Heaven,' *Oxford Book of English Verse*, Granada Publishing, 1900, p. 1079.
3. Ven. Ian Jagger, Sermon in Durham Cathedral, 2003.
4. Matthew 13:44–46.
5. Carol Shields, *Unless*, Fourth Estate, 2002, p. 56.
6. Philip Sheldrake, *Befriending our Desires*, DLT, 2001, p. 33.
7. Henri Nouwen, *The Inner Voice of Love*, DLT, 1996, p. 3.
8. St Augustine of Hippo (354–430).
9. C. S. Lewis, *The Four Loves*, HarperCollins, 1960, p. 116.
10. Luke 10:27.
11. Psalm 27:8, Revised Standard Version.
12. Luke 3:22.
13. R. S. Thomas, *Collected Poems 1945–1990*, Phoenix Press, 1993, p. 364.
14. Anonymous, chapter 75, *The Cloud of Unknowing, (HarperCollins Spiritual Classics),* HarperCollins San Francisco, 2004, p. 148.

Reflection 3: The Gifts of Forgiveness

1. John 7:53–8:11.
2. John 8:7.
3. John V. Taylor, *The Christlike God*, SCM Press, 1992, p. 202. I

am greatly indebted to John V. Taylor for this quotation which has informed much of my thinking in this reflection, 'It is hard for anyone who makes a principle of avoiding pain or reactively paying it back on someone else to understand what forgiveness means, and aggressively independent natures cannot conceive of the miracle whereby one who pardons an injury contains the sting and outrage of it in the hope of preserving the relationship at any cost and turning an evil act into an occasion of greater good. Yet this is what the self-giving God has always done.'

4. Desmund Tutu, *No Future Without Forgiveness*, Rider, 1999, p. 228.
5. The Archbishops' Council, *Common Worship*, Church House Publishing, 2000, p. 170.
6. Mark Barrett, *Crossing*, DLT, 2001, p. 57. Quoting Anthony Minghella, *The Talented Mr Ripley*, a screenplay based on the novel by Patricia Highsmith (London: Methuen, 2000, pp. 114–115).
7. Clarissa Pinkola Estes, *Women Who Run With the Wolves*, Rider, 1992, p. 375.
8. C. S. Lewis, 'On Forgiveness', *Fern-Seed and Elephants and Other Essays*, HarperCollins, 1975, p. 26.
9. John V. Taylor, p. 202.
10. Dag Hammarskjöld, *Markings*, Faber and Faber, 1964, p. 163.
11. Matthew 18:23–35.
12. Luke 10:27.
13. Matthew 6:12.
14. Exodus 20:5.
15. Jonathan Baker, *How Forgiveness Works*, 1995, Grove Books, p. 14.
16. Matthew 20:1–16.
17. Matthew 20:16.
18. Matthew 16:5–12.
19. John 21:15–17.
20. John V. Taylor, p. 202.
21. ibid.

Reflection 4: Paying Attention

1. Rainer Maria Rilke quoted in Michael Mayne, *The Sunrise of Wonder*, Fount, 1995, p. 123.
2. Brian Keenan, *An Evil Cradling*, Vintage Books, 1993, p. 68.
3. Romans 1:19–20
4. Alice Walker, *The Color Purple*, The Women's Press, 1983, p. 167.
5. Donald Nicholl, *Holiness*, DLT, 1981, p. 72.
6. Anthony de Mello, *The Song of the Bird*, Doubleday, 1982, pp. 72–73.
7. Philip Toynbee, *Part of a Journey*, Collins, 1981, p. 139.
8. Alan McGlashan quoted in Francis Dewar, *Invitations*, SPCK, 1996, p. 37.
9. Luke 10:27.
10. Iris Murdoch, *The Sovereignty of Good*, Routledge, 1978, p. 68.
11. John V. Taylor, *The Christlike God*, SCM, 1992, p. 276.
12. ibid.
13. Kat Duff, *The Alchemy of Illness*, Virago, 1994, p. 43.
14. Donald Nicholl, *Holiness*, DLT, 1981, p. 77.
15. Mark 1:21–34.
16. Colossians 1:19.
17. Rowan Williams, *Lecture*, Holy Rood House, Thirsk, 7 February, 2003.
18. R. S. Thomas, *Collected Poems*, Phoenix Press, 1995, p. 302.

Reflection 5: Friendship

1. Elisabeth Schussler Fiorenza, *In Memory of Her: A Feminist Reconstruction of Christian Origins*, SCM, 1983, p. 345.
2. Alan Boesak, *Black and Reformed*, Orbis Books, 1984, p. 51.
3. Mark Oakley, *The Collage of God*, DLT, 2001, p. 79.
4. St Augustine of Hippo (354–430), Sermon 80 on the New Testament.
5. David Ford, *The Shape of Living*, Fount, 1997, p. 4.
6. Trevor Dennis, *Face to Face with God*, SPCK, 1999, p. 83.

7. Robert Fyall, *How Does God Treat His Friends?*, Christian Focus Publications, 1995, p. 48.
8. Trevor Dennis, p. 85.
9. Margaret Silf, *Landmarks*, DLT, 1998, p. 251.
10. Harper Lee, *To Kill a Mockingbird*, William Heinemann, 1960, p. 35.
11. Thomas W. Ogletree, *Hospitality to the Stranger*, Fortress Press, 1985, pp. 2–3.
12. Paul J. Wadell, *Friendship in the Moral Life*, University of Notre Dame Press, 1989, p. 152.
13. Paul J. Wadell, p. 159.
14. John 15:15.
15. Luke 22:39–46.
16. Matthew 26:50.
17. Ruth Etchells, *The Rainbow Coloured Cross* (to be published by SPCK, 2007).
18. Adrian Thatcher, *Liberating Sex: A Christian Sexual Theology*, SPCK, 1993, p. 55.

Reflection 6: Success and Failure

1. Henri Nouwen, *In the Name of Jesus*, Crossroad, 1989, p. 10.
2. Mark 8:36, *The Message Bible*, NavPress, 2003.
3. Matthew 4:1–11.
4. Mark 10:17.
5. Mark 10:21.
6. Mark 10:46–52.
7. I want to acknowledge and thank Richard Rohr for helping me to see these well-known passages in a new way. Richard Rohr, *Simplicity*, Crossroad, 1991, pp. 137–144.
8. Rudyard Kipling, 'If', *Rudyard Kipling's Verse*, Hodder and Stoughton, 1940, p. 576.
9. Henri Nouwen, *In the Name of Jesus*, DLT, 1989, pp. 15–16.
10. Luke 24:13–35.
11. Ralph Wright, 'Two Trees' quoted in Maria Boulding, *Gateway*

to Hope, Fount, 1985, p. 72.

12. Matthew 13:24–30, New Revised Standard Version, DLT, 2005.
13. 2 Samuel 11–12, ibid.
14. 2 Samuel 12:1–6, ibid.
15. 2 Samuel 12:5 New International Version, Hodder & Stoughton, 1979.
16. Luke 11:4, NRSV.
17. 2 Samuel 12:13, NRSV.
18. 2 Samuel 12:15–23, NRSV.
19. Matthew 16:16, NRSV.
20. Luke 22:31–34, NRSV.
21. Luke 22:32, NRSV.
22. Richard Rohr, ibid. p. 64.
23. Ann Lewin, *Watching for the Kingfisher* (Inspire, an imprint of Methodist Publishing House).